Over 40 Women Share Their Inspiring Stories of Stepping into Courage, Leading from the Heart, and Personal Evolution

THE DECONSTRUCTING G.R.I.T. COLLECTION

Growth

COMPILED BY
JENNIFER BARDOT

GROWTH - Deconstructing GRIT Collection
Over 40 women share their inspiring stories of stepping into courage, leading from the heart and personal evolution
MDC Press

Published by **MDC Press**, St. Louis, MO
Copyright ©2022
All rights reserved.

Cover, Interior Design, and Project Management:
  Davis Creative Publishing Partners, CreativePublishingPartners.com
Writing Coach and Editor: Maria Rodgers O'Rourke

Compilation by Jennifer Bardot

Library of Congress Cataloging-in-Publication Data (Produced by Cassidy Cataloguing Services, Inc.)

Names: Bardot, Jennifer, compiler.
Title: Growth : the deconstructing G.R.I.T. collection / compiled by Jennifer Bardot.
Other titles: Growth GRIT
Description: St. Louis, MO : MDC Press, [2022]
Identifiers: ISBN: 978-1-7371848-2-9 (paperback) | 978-1-7371848-3-6 (ebook) | LCCN: 2022910195
Subjects: LCSH: Self-actualization (Psychology) in women--Literary collections. | Self-actualization (Psychology) in women--Anecdotes. | Maturation (Psychology)--Literary collections. | Maturation (Psychology)--Anecdotes. | Courage--Literary collections. | Courage--Anecdotes. | Resilience (Personality trait)--Literary collections. | Resilience (Personality trait)-- Anecdotes. | LCGFT: Anecdotes.
Classification: LCC: BF637.S4 G76 2022 | DDC: 158.1--dc23

I dedicate this book to my family
and all my dear friends who
have supported, believed in, and
inspired me to GROW.
Thank you for helping me develop
into the woman I am today.

TABLE OF CONTENTS

Jennifer Bardot

Introduction

This book is meant to inspire and empower readers to GROW as individuals, professionals and as members of the community at large.

Through real-life stories of over 40 women featured in this collection provide life-lessons and encouragement that feed the soul and enrich the development of others.

While the pace and speed of GROWTH is unique to each person, the paths that lead to it tend to cross one another and share some key elements.

As readers take a brief walk in the shoes of these remarkable leaders, they will soon find themselves envisioning ways to follow in their footsteps and cultivate the fully developed lives they wish to live.

Jennifer Bardot

Challenge Accepted

"Change is inevitable. Growth is optional."
– John Maxwell

Growth begins with a choice. We must choose to believe in our self-worth and ability to achieve our goals when faced with challenges. It is a choice between merely talking about overcoming challenges and deliberately acting to overcome them. Less talking, more doing is real growth. Many people listen to and read self-help books and are motivated in the moment by "gurus," but in the end **we** must choose to invite change.

For me, that choice was to believe I had value beyond my current circumstances and to embrace an "I can" mindset. My journey, which will not end until my final breath, began with a desire to test my capabilities and to embrace challenges. Trying something new is scary. In my teens, I went cliff jumping. Peering over the edge, I was nervous and scared…but after the plunge I felt a rush of adrenaline and couldn't wait to do it again! I could have focused on all the things that could go wrong, or I could leap off fearlessly and torpedo into the lake. I chose to jump and be fearless!

Being cautious helps us survive as humans, but through taking chances, branching out, and innovating, we have enabled ourselves to evolve and advance as a species. By trying new things, facing new challenges, we test our capacity, learn, and modify. When things don't go as we expect, we learn the most about ourselves.

Real growth starts when you begin calling yourself out and correcting yourself. Instead of blaming others, you take your power back by being responsible for your life.

"We can't afford to keep you." These are the words I heard one week after giving birth to my second child. My position was eliminated when the "Pancake Year" began. Mine was the only source of income for my family, I didn't have a plan B. Heck, I hadn't even recovered from having a baby. I felt helpless, unprepared, and embarrassed. I look back on the "Pancake Year" after eating pancakes for every almost meal, and now I am grateful for its lessons. It taught me how much I valued family, that money comes and goes, and that I can do hard things. Choosing to live in a foundation of gratitude and faith invited hope into these stressful times and reminded me of my strength. During this time, I struggled alone and didn't share with my friends or ask for support. My embarrassment from my circumstances caused me to shut down being vulnerable fearing judgement by those closest to me. I've grown from this carb-loaded year and retrained my brain to be vulnerable with those I trust and have no fear of being embarrassed.

When you forgive, you heal. When you let go, you grow. We have the power to make these choices to heal and grow. When we are dealt a bad hand, we can't fold. We must keep playing the game of life. Experiencing wins and losses helps us gain confidence. Confidence leads to more advanced challenges, and challenges lead to more experiences. This cycle drives growth based on choices, mindset, and actions. I have experienced this cycle many times in my life, and typically catalyzed my growth through a major life event or from moments of stress, struggle, change, transition and stepping out of my comfort zone. These moments provide us with an opportunity to learn something new about ourselves when faced with an unexpected challenge.

Not all growth is intentional; oftentimes it happens without our knowledge. Children, for example, are constantly growing from trying new things and overcoming failures. When I first learned to drive, I had several accidents… much to my parents' distress. I was scared, but I still got in that driver's seat and tried again. In 3rd grade I fell off a train at an amusement park and was nearly run over. My parents still refuse to discuss what happened because the incident was so traumatic for our family. This accident forever heightened my awareness of my surroundings and taught me to take responsibility for my own safety. Years later, harboring a lot of fear, I chose to return to the park. My father, on the other hand, has never returned to the park, nor will he talk about the mental image he has of seeing his daughter laying on train tracks of a bridge with a 50-foot drop off to the rocks below.

Talk about feelings? Nope, not how I was raised. My father is an amazing dad, grandfather, friend, and mentor. He has taught me many valuable lessons…but talking about trauma ain't one of them. He was a bricklayer and stonemason by trade until his retirement from his family company, George McDonnell & Sons. He won numerous safety awards over the years. Since we do not discuss the incident at the park, I do not know if it influenced his mindset on the importance of safety. However, I can't help but think it had some impact and helped him to grow into the safety-conscious man he is today. But growth is a personal journey, so I cannot speak for him. While my growth came years later when I returned to the park, his experience may have impacted him more immediately. The point is that growth is different for everyone, even when they experience the same event. How you choose to grow, if at all, is up to you.

Since I was a young child, I have pushed the limits and rules, speaking up when something wasn't right, and doing things even when I was told

I couldn't. I had a big mouth and heart, and I was head strong (I still do and I still am!). Choosing to push limits, do hard things, and follow my gut has enabled my self-discovery with lots of courageous wounds along the way. I was limiting myself if I always did what was easy, or what other people expected of me. Ditching the negative head trash, changing, recognizing my capacity is how I began to level up and transform my life.

From my experience, everything is hard before it is easy. It is easier to stop dreaming, reading, and improving, but studies support that reading is significantly better for building connections within our brains. Our brains grow by doing what is hard, just as our muscles grow by doing what is hard. To grow as humans, we must choose to stop doing what is easy. I was the first person on either side of my family to graduate from college. I then chose to go to graduate school and obtain two master's degrees, making the dean's list while also choosing to work sixty-hour weeks across two jobs. My educational experience significantly improved my work ethic, multi-tasking, and confidence in my abilities to manage my schedule and life.

According to the *Harvard Business Review*, people can train their brains to focus on the positive. Training for positivity is all about muscle memory. The brain, even in adulthood, is continuously developing though our actions and behaviors. We can deliberately wire our brains for optimism and build beneficial habits that enable growth. These actions lead to increased optimism and life satisfaction: writing a positive message, meditating, exercising, journaling, and practicing gratitude. Creating new habits will yield a new outcome. As is often (mis)attributed to Albert Einstein, "The definition of insanity is doing the same thing over and over again and expecting a different result."

Whatever makes YOU uncomfortable is your opportunity for growth. Recently, I chose to leave a successful career for an entirely different industry, which was an extremely difficult decision but an opportunity to push myself to higher levels. Many people could not believe it, but I knew that by doing what was hard I was going to learn, fight, adapt, and ultimately grow to new levels, further advancing my belief in myself. Every choice I have made up to this point in my life has been the "hard choice," and as a result I have grown exponentially in self-awareness.

My friends, families, and those in the community who know me well often ask how I can manage a career, book, family, speaking engagements, volunteer work, mentorships, etc. This is not an easy balancing act, nor was the path to get here. I took risks, stumbled over obstacles, suffered painful failures, navigated financial hardships, and cried when I suffered personal losses. Unfortunately, we all experience some, if not all, of these hardships in our lifetime. But choosing to do what is hard instead of easy has helped me cope with these very difficult times in my life because I believe in myself and know what I can do. I can bounce back, I have mental toughness, but I wasn't born that strong. I built my mental toughness through experiencing failure, taking risks, and taking one step at a time pushing ahead. I am unapologetically who I am. I am bold, I am aware of my faults, and I care deeply for others. I choose to walk with courage and passion even if it leads to failures and heartache. It's my choice.

"You are who you associate with" is a saying of my family. I choose to surround myself with dreamers, doers, believers, thinkers, trend-setters, and cycle-breakers—and you will read these women's stories in the *Deconstructing G.R.I.T. Collection.* These women tell their stories of courage and growth in the hope that their experiences become part of someone else's survival guide. Self-development is a personal journey; only you are the captain. Yours will be a different journey than mine, but I hope you choose growth.

Never limit your growth. It is not a one-size-fits-all approach. Maybe you will be inspired and develop your own steps to grow from these stories, Maybe you won't. But as you read these words, recognize that you have already made a choice to walk alongside the authors in this book. I thank you for making that choice to read these women's personal journeys of growth.

CHALLENGE:

Imagine the person YOU want to be. Visualize the daily life, habits, and routines for your future self. Start showing up as who you envision, implement the habits and routines, and start building. Step by step, day by day, with each deliberate choice you make to grow, you are transforming into the person YOU want to be.

Jennifer Bardot is a publisher and author of the *Deconstructing G.R.I.T. Collection* and *Owning Your G.R.I.T.*, an international best-selling anthology found in Target, Walmart, Barnes and Noble, and everywhere books are sold. She earned her B.A. in Business Administration and holds dual Master's Degrees in Secondary Education and Private Practice Therapy. Jennifer holds certifications from Dare to Lead, Leadership St. Louis by Focus St. Louis, and is a member of the 72nd class of Coro Women in Leadership.

Jennifer is a Consultant for Health and Benefits for Willis Towers Watson and is a member of Willis Towers Watson's SHE Leads Program for 2022. In 2021, Jennifer was featured on the cover of *St. Louis Small Business Monthly* as one of the "Top 100 People to Know to Help Grow Your Business." Formerly with Enterprise Bank & Trust, she earned recognition both as a Top Business Banker six months into her banking career and as a member of the President's Circle.

Jennifer is also the co-founder of Thought Partners, a women's business community with over 450 members. She volunteers much of her time with startup ecosystems and non-profits, including service as the Chair of CycleNation American Heart Association. She is a dedicated mother of 3 and an outdoor adrenaline adventurer.

www.linkedin.com/company/deconstructinggritseries/?viewAsMember=true
www.linkedin.com/in/jennifer-mcdonnell-bardot/
www.facebook.com/DECONSTRUCTINGGRIT

Brandy Scheer

Matriarchs, Motherhood, and Mentoring

Of all the things I wanted to be when I grew up, the one thing I instinctively knew I would become, no matter what profession I chose, was a mother.

A passion to nurture, teach, lead, protect, encourage, and support all those around me was instilled within me from the very beginning. My mother and grandmother, who have always served as role models, inspired me to continuously strive for excellence at every stage and in every aspect of my life. Deep down, I have always known that dedicating myself to a life of continual growth would equip me to raise children, help my community thrive, and ultimately lead and mentor others.

"I see trees of green, red roses too, I see them bloom for me and you, and I think to myself, what a wonderful world…I hear babies cry, I watch them grow, they'll learn much more than I'll ever know, and I think to myself, what a wonderful world."

Louis Armstrong's lyrics would emanate from my minivan radio every weekday right as I pulled into the long carpool line at my son's preschool. The song signified the end of a local morning radio show. Hearing the life-affirming verses and belting out the words together soon became a time-honored tradition for my son and me. Having already developed a keen sense of humor, my little guy would always shout out a big "whaaaa" right after he sang the "babies cry" part. It did not matter that we were both well aware of his impending joke. This simple shared ritual made us laugh every time and helped us begin each day on a high note.

Back in those days, we could not fathom how much that song would come to mean us both. We did not analyze its significance or break down the meaning behind the melody. We just thought it was fun.

Now, however, it is crystal clear that "What a Wonderful World" was and still is an anthem about growing up. To this day, whenever we hear it, we realize how much has changed, how we've both grown personally and professionally, and how important those sing-alongs were to the evolution of who we are today.

By sharing such beautiful underlying statements day in and day out, I believe we were both intrinsically learning and reinforcing life's most important, foundational lessons:

- Value the world you live in and all that surrounds you.
- Love people unconditionally, embrace their differences, and appreciate what makes them unique.
- Learn that family, friendship, and connectivity with others is what life is all about.

Once I made the commitment to writing a chapter for this book, I became overwhelmed by the numerous directions my portion of this anthology could take. Should I write about the best practices I learned throughout my professional career that led me from one incredible role to the next? Should I talk about how the loss of my mother almost destroyed me but has now helped me grow stronger than I ever thought possible? What aspects of my life, literally and figuratively, represent growth, and which ones would be most beneficial to share with readers? Upon careful reflection, I decided to write about three ideas to answer all those questions.

Matriarchs

A matriarch is defined as a woman who rules or dominates a family, group, or state. When referenced in literature or pop culture, the term often conjures opposite images of either elderly, refined grandmothers who preside as the grandames of highbrow, elite families, or powerful, superheroine, warrior goddesses like those portrayed in Greek mythology or in DC's Wonder Woman, Amazonian world.

Functioning matriarchal societies with women at the helm, though rare, do exist in the world today.

But when I think of a matriarch, I think of those women—and there seems to be one in every family—who not only care for and run their own households but who end up either taking on or acquiring family responsibilities cast upon them by others.

These are the women of the "sandwich generation" who must physically, financially and/or emotionally support aging parents and relatives, children of all ages, and sometimes even grandchildren, nieces, and nephews while they simultaneously maintain meaningful marriages/partnerships, careers that crash through glass ceilings, and their own physical/mental strength.

There are also matriarchs who have led and inspired countless groups of women by simply living their lives and standing up for what they believe to be true. Historically, ladies like Marie Curie, Amelia Earhart, Rosa Parks, and Queen Elizabeth paved the way for more contemporary powerful women like Ruth Bader Ginsburg, Golda Meir, Gloria Steinem, Hillary Clinton, and Oprah Winfrey, and so many others who change our world for the better.

What these matriarchs have in common, and why I think all matriarchs represent growth, is that each clearly valued what the worlds they lived in had to offer, loved and cared for others so they too could grow and develop into their best selves, and understood that relationships and a sense of community define the meaning of life.

Motherhood

Nothing, absolutely nothing in life, has taught me more about growth than motherhood.

From the time I was born, and I am guessing even while I was in utero, my mother is without a doubt the person who most influenced, shaped, cultivated, encouraged, and enhanced who I was at any given time and who I would become as an adult. Like those previously mentioned, she and my grandmother were matriarchs. Each was the glue that held their families and everyone who touched their lives together.

As the baton passed from one to the other, each placed their useful knowledge and experiences in a carefully crafted, gigantic life-skills toolbox that they lovingly passed on to me. I have opened that box, shared its contents, and will one day hopefully pass it along to my daughter, but only after adding a few of my own secrets to it.

Key lessons found in that magical kit have served me well in both my personal and professional life. Among them: Never burn a bridge; make friends with everyone at every level within an organization and respect them all equally; all people are just people, so there is no need be afraid to talk to someone; ask nicely for what you want and you will most likely get it; always lift people up, especially when they are struggling, and you can often accomplish that with nothing more than a smile; and surrounding yourself with people who have a positive outlook and who love you for who you are will enable you to accomplish even your wildest dreams.

While I certainly do not consider myself an expert on the topic of growth, I do know that quite a bit of it takes place in a blink of an eye. As a mom, when you turn around and see your youngest child, your baby girl, the one who wore frilly doll-like dresses and matching black patent leather shoes, graduating college, you know her growing up has happened much too fast. The melody of "Sunrise, Sunset" from *Fiddler on the Roof* floats through my mind: "Is this the little girl I carried?" Wasn't it yesterday that she was coloring with crayons, playing with dolls, and cuddling up with me to hear bedtime stories?

Despite this phenomenon, I also remember those times when I felt like my kids were never going to grow up. I was certainly thinking that during the sweltering month of August when I was eight-months pregnant and begging for that September baby to be born. I definitely felt that way when I was potty training my kids, dealing with tantrums at the grocery store, and when my five-year-old hid in the middle of a circular clothing rack and my heart stopped for what felt like an eternity but quickly started again when I heard him giggling and he poked his little face out between the dresses.

Mentoring

For those who never want to stop developing personally or professionally, mentoring may be the perfect path to continued growth. In such a dynamic relationship, the advantages to the mentee are somewhat obvious. But what, may you ask, is in it for the mentor?

Technological advances and industry standards are changing at the speed of light. Those of us who no longer earn continuing education credits or who have not seen a classroom in quite some time, now have a unique opportunity to create relationships where learning, inspiration, and career development flow in both directions.

Just as matriarchs and mothers have always shaped the next generation, we as mentors can have a real impact on flowering the future. We have the opportunity not only to help greener, less-experienced individuals blossom but to help them better understand that growth is a lifelong process. Our stories clearly demonstrate valuable and unforgettable transformative lessons while our roots and experience can stabilize the seeds of the future.

Brandy Scheer is the enthusiastic, results-oriented owner and CEO of Scheer Resources. Her passion is helping business owners simplify their lives through efficient, combined BD/Marketing Strategic Plans.

After receiving her bachelor's degree in journalism/marketing from KU, Brandy went on to work for communications giant FleishmanHillard, as well as with multiple publications including the *St. Louis Post-Dispatch*, *St. Louis Magazine*, *Ladue News*, *CNR*, and *St. Louis Design Magazine*.

"Recruited" to serve as the Department of Defense's Missouri ESGR executive director, Brandy also led both state and national military employer relations programs.

As the marketing director for several architect, engineering, and construction firms, most of Brandy's thirty-plus-year professional career has been in the A/E/C industry. Currently on the Dean's Advisory Committee for Harris-Stowe's Anheuser-Busch School of Business, Brandy is also a board member with Hope Creates and PEOPLE of Construction, and is the Membership/Emerging Leaders Chair for the St. Louis Council of Construction Consumers.

www.linkedin.com/in/brandyscheer/
www.scheerresources.com/

Debbie Novak

Embracing My Journey

"A journey is a person in itself; no two are alike."
-John Steinbeck

When you think of a personal journey of growth, what comes to your mind? Everyone's answers will vary because everyone's journey is different. Each is unique and special. However, our journeys are no more important than the next person's. As women, we all have stages in our lives that contribute to this journey. Our journey may change as our priorities and circumstances change and as we age and mature. For me, my journey can be summed up in three major categories: Professional Growth, Growing through Motherhood, and Personal Growth.

I started with our parent company, Lionmark Construction Cos., when I was nineteen. I have been here for twenty-seven years. Since 2015, I have worked for Missouri Petroleum Products, which is a company under the Lionmark umbrella. With each position I have held, I have always tried to learn more and make myself available for professional growth. I have never turned down a new opportunity. Even if I knew nothing about it and was nervous, I knew I would learn and give it my best. As a result of many opportunities, I have a well-rounded knowledge of this company and how things work. I am proud to be a part of this company, and I am grateful for the opportunities they have allowed and the trust they bestow on me.

In my current position, I sell asphalt maintenance products and purchase the liquid asphalt used to make our products. The liquid asphalt is the most expensive component in everything we make. My employer trusts my instincts, knowledge, and decision-making in this process. I take this trust seriously and deeply appreciate it.

I love the variety my job offers. I love networking and getting to know new people. I have made cherished, forever friends from this industry. The asphalt industry is predominantly male. In 2019, I was asked to serve on the board of directors for Women of Asphalt. This is a national organization that supports, educates, and advocates for women in the industry. It has been a privilege to be a part of this organization and has helped grow my network even further. I serve as Chairwoman for the Missouri Branch of Women of Asphalt. We have a group consisting of smart and talented women. This branch is affiliated with and aided by the Missouri Asphalt Pavement Association (MAPA). I love the talented women I now call my friends, and how we help each other grow, support each other, and encourage young women to pursue a career in this industry. It is refreshing to attend conferences and see more female faces in the crowd. This industry is progressive and forward thinking. The support from men for Women of Asphalt has been wonderful to experience.

When I started as receptionist at this company twenty-seven years ago, I could not have imagined I would be serving on the board for a national women's organization! I am proud of my professional growth.

"A mother's love liberates."

-Maya Angelou

In 2007, my son, Conner, was born. He is my biggest and best achievement. I am sure every mother feels this way! At fifteen, he calls me his best friend. That humbles me so much. He is kind, thoughtful, respectful, self-aware, mature beyond his age, and very patient. He very rarely loses his temper or reacts in anger. His level of self-control is amazing. He blows fifteen-year-old me out of the water! To say I am proud to be his mother is greatly understated. I look forward to watching his journey continue into adulthood and becoming a wonderful father. Many, many years from now, I hope!

My son has helped me grow. He has helped me see the person I want to be and to set a good example for him. He has shown me what is exceptionally important in life and that moments of joy are free. Children do not need expensive toys or all the latest trends to make them happy. Our presence and stability are what sustains them. I am thankful for the times he puts his phone away and sits with me to talk or play games/cards. Those are moments I do not turn down, because one day he will be out on his own and those moments will become fewer and farther between. Those are moments I will never get back. I have learned to take a breath and soak them in.

"Change is inevitable but personal growth is a choice."

-Bob Proctor

This statement is both profound and accurate.

In reflecting on my personal growth for this book, I realize that I am in a constant state of metamorphosis. I have had many stages in my life. Some not so good. There have been times I was not the best person. All my life, I have struggled with deep insecurities. I was angry and reacted irrationally to situations, often in an unkind way. I look back and am not proud of some past behavior. But everything I have done has led me to the person I am now. I am the best version of me!

My professional experiences of taking on new opportunities made me realize this: Change is scary. It is uncertain. Just because you take a leap does not mean you will land on both feet every time. No one truly learns without the lessons offered by failure. I had to harness that professional courage into my personal life. We are never too old to change and to pursue our happiness. Unfortunately, there were many people in my life who were unaccepting of the changes I made. As a result, I have lost many people I love. I know they love me and think they are doing the loving thing by cutting me out of their lives. I still love them, and I am not angry or mad at them for this. But my biggest challenge in change has been *me*. My insecurities were still holding me back. Every time I took one step forward, I would also take three steps back and revert to unhealthy behaviors, contrary to growth. I did not feel strong, confident, or sure of myself the way I did professionally or as a mother. So I spent some time reflecting on why this was. That process led me to make the biggest change in my life yet.

When I was six years old, I was taken advantage of by an older boy. This happened in my home, in my bedroom closet. I could hear my parents and his parents downstairs talking and having fun. My protectors were so close but unreachable. It was terrifying and the most traumatic event in my life. I kept that secret for twelve years and lived with it on my own. Because I had no counseling, my means of escape and ways of dealing with the issues stemming from the abuse were unhealthy and further damaging. But in my time of self-reflection, I discovered this: that six-year-old little girl was brave enough and smart enough to *never let it happen again*. He tried. Several times. But she never allowed herself to be alone with him or be out of sight from an adult or other people when he was near. That little girl was *strong*!

During this time of self-reflection, I discovered that strength is still in me. I found my confidence and self-worth. I found *me*. It was the most liberated I have ever felt! That little girl had been inside of me for forty years screaming to get out! When released, I could hear her voice telling me: "It is about time!"

I no longer feel controlled by my insecurities and my emotions. I feel empowered. Renewed. I feel happy being me, just as I am. I have worked toward being a better mother, woman, friend, and human. I am confident knowing I am a good person and have a good heart. I now choose to take the "high road" instead of engaging in confrontations and anger. It is easier to be kind than it is to be mean. It takes so much effort and energy to be mean. It is exhausting and never worth it in the end.

I no longer seek the approval of others to make me feel accepted. If people who have known us for so long stop "liking" us because of our choices, is that our problem or theirs? Harnessing the inner strength and power it takes to genuinely not care what others think of you, and not allowing their opinions to shape your choices, is empowering. Again, I love the ones I have lost and miss them terribly, but during this journey I have renewed and gained friendships. I have friends in my life who are like family. They accept me for me, just as I am. That is unconditional love, and it is an incredibly beautiful experience. I am so grateful for them!

It is never too late to change. It is never too late to be happy. Find your strength and tap into it. You will never regret it.

Embrace *your* journey!

Debbie Novak started with Missouri Petroleum's parent company, Lionmark Construction Cos., LLC, in September 1995. Currently, Debbie is responsible for the Company's Asphalt Purchasing, managing the Company's asphalt needs for emulsions and cutbacks. In addition, she oversees the marketing for every Lionmark company and maintains all individual websites and social media for each.

Debbie is a member of APWA (American Public Works Association) Missouri Chapter and is involved with other organizations such as AGC (American General Contractors) of Missouri, SITE and MAPA (Missouri Asphalt Pavement Association).

Debbie currently serves on the Board of Directors for Women of Asphalt which is a national organization for women in the asphalt industry. The organization's goals are:

AWARENESS - Increasing awareness of opportunities in the industry.
KNOWLEDGE - Elevating knowledge through education and resources.
COMMUNITY - Providing platforms to create supportive relationships and growth.

Debbie also serves as Chairwoman for Women of Asphalt, Missouri Branch.

Debbie is a proud mother to her teenage son, Conner, and currently resides in Wentzville, Missouri. She loves to spend time with her son playing cards, games and going to Cardinals and Blues games together. She loves to attend Pilates weekly and tries to stay active.

www.linkedin.com/in/debbie-novak-21854036/

Kelly Reid Jackson

Listening, Learning, and Leveraging Growth

Growth happens each and every day for most of us. Opportunities for listening, self-development, vocational training, and learning from others have all been critical elements to building growth for me.

I was shy and insecure in middle school. Maybe you can relate? I was too shy to answer the teacher's question when I knew the answer. I didn't like being this way, so I joined show choir, entered a dance contest, performed a gymnastics routine in front of the entire school, and ran for student body president. I went for it and pushed myself. I was fortunate to have a mother who taught me to be a go-getter. I wanted her to be proud of me!

I didn't win student body president. I fell in the dance contest, slipping on the floor, and my bra strap broke during the gymnastic routine. Show choir was a success, although I was not the best singer by any means. I grew with each of these experiences, though, and had I never tried them, I wouldn't have gained anything.

Throughout school, I kept going, learning, and leading in various ways. I was even chosen by the school district as one of two for a leadership summer camp after my freshman year in high school. This was my first taste of leadership and growth. I can't say I listened to all the advice.

For example, my natural gifts were apparently in business and marketing, according to my business teacher. I earned a school award for business, and he strongly suggested I go to business school. But I decided I knew better and chose a legal career. I was too stubborn to really listen and appreciate the gift he was offering. He was much wiser and more knowledgeable than me. Sometimes it's too difficult to see in yourself what others do. Heck, I even participated in teaching middle schoolers business and still didn't get it! Perhaps I was a typical teenager? Go figure.

It's so much easier to reflect on forty-nine years and pick up on all the signs that could have directed my path or simply guided it. Luckily, I learned to really listen to others early in adulthood. Making many mistakes can open your ears and mind to realize you are growing. I have come to see, however, that there is growth and there is asserted growth. As a career marketing professional, I would be remiss to not recognize the importance of planning, research, analysis, and continuing education.

I had a plan to educate myself while going to school. My plan lacked some important data and research, though. I didn't meet an attorney before I worked for one. I didn't understand the day-to-day job of a para-legal or an attorney. I saw them on TV like everyone else. But did I really know the job? I didn't know how to really evaluate myself to best under-stand if I was meant to do that sort of work. Sure, I could learn, but was it me? I learned through trial and error. I loved legal knowledge but didn't like the tedious aspects of the work or the specific challenges of legalities. I like fun, I like competition, I love design, and I am a huge people person who enjoys a great conversation. Well, for me, being a paralegal didn't equate to any of these. But marketing did.

When I finally set on the right path, I engrossed myself in better under-standing my talents, preferences, and needs. This is when the asserted growth I mentioned changed *everything*. Instead of growth happening through passive learning and half listening, I made growth intentional. I completed my Bachelor of Arts in Advertising, Marketing, and Media Communications. The accomplishment was encouraged by some of the best advice from a former supervisor who led client relations at the biggest law firm in St. Louis. Again, getting the right direction means you need to seek it out. I simply asked, "How can I grow in marketing?"

I worked full time at age nineteen and went to school full time as well. Working in my field and leveraging my talents afforded me knowledge and skills beyond my years. One year after graduation, I was a marketing coordinator and the only one in the marketing department for the local offices of the biggest engineering firm in the world. I took it all in. I challenged myself in a technical industry by listening to everyone around me, the engineers, and colleagues from other firms. They all mentored me in marketing for the architectural, engineering, and construction industry. I took initiative to join a national marketing organization for professional services dedicated to the natural and built environment. I even jumped on their board immediately as the Sponsorship Chair. I later leveraged those relationships as I chased projects and needed to build teams, and to build myself. Again, I sought mentors. There were plenty of people who knew a lot more than I did about the industry. I took the time and the opportunity to learn all I could. I grew because I chose asserted growth.

The organization offered a plethora of resources, ongoing training and education, and contacts. I read just about every book available, and I went to all the local educational programs and to many national conferences. Within two years on the board, I became President Elect. I leveraged this to grow not only my company's visibility but my own too. I believed it was in everyone's best interest that I know as many people as possible for partnering, for learning about clients and opportunities, and for overall relationships.

I mentioned earlier I was shy. I was not an extrovert, and I was insecure. Instead of giving in to this, I took many steps to combat the nerves and insecurities. I accepted what I couldn't change and changed what I could. Yes, that is a part of the Serenity Prayer. If you read the Serenity Prayer from start to finish, it's great advice. Change what you can and stop agonizing over what you can't. This has been essential in my day-to-day life. I will get to that in a bit. I overcame so much shyness. I didn't say earlier that I even got into theater in school and in mock trial. Both were scary as you-know-what, but I loved them so much! And I became a much more confident and stronger person.

In my career, I eventually led several marketing departments and was director of business development. I'm a central part of the construction industry. I gained a lot of skills working in marketing, as many of us do, and took a break from being employed to being self-employed. I started my own marketing, design, and web agency, which I ran for eight years. I took all that listening and learning and leveraged it into an agency I knew would be unique due to my professional services expertise. I leveraged the skills learned on-the-job as well as some from school. And I went for it. I helped over one hundred and fifty companies, including many start-ups and mostly small businesses with less than $5 million in revenue. I again listened to as many advisors as I could and learned all about running a business as well as the latest in technology and digital marketing strategies. I leveraged the relationships I forged in the design and construction industry to build my initial base of clients, but knew I needed to diversify my target audience to strengthen my business.

I also needed to fill my toolbox, including all the resources any business owner requires to be successful. I needed an accountant and tax preparer as well as a corporate attorney, IT support, video production company, photographer, illustrator, web developers, and business consultants and coaches. There were more, but these were key for me. Like before, I knew I needed to acquire more knowledge and forge more relationships to build my new business. So, of course, I joined the local chamber and a networking group. I worked on all three: listening, learning, and leveraging (my three Ls).

Today, I run a fifty-one-year-old construction organization comprised of the largest companies and governments in town as well as many diverse and smaller companies—about one hundred and seventy-eight organization members. It's the St. Louis Council of Construction Consumers (SLC3), and all roads and all implementation of my 3 Ls led here. This role taps into my best talents and brings me to the biggest career purpose for my life. As a woman in a male-dominated industry, it feels especially empowering to lead such a meaningful organization with so many truly inspiring people who shape our built/natural environment. As the Executive Director, I lead us in technology, continuing education, diversity/equity/inclusion, and in collaboration while leveraging those marketing, legal, and PR talents and strengths. I never expected to be in this role; however, with an asserted effort to learn and grow, I am making a positive impact to improve our region. Amen to growth!

Kelly Reid Jackson is Executive Director of the St. Louis Council of Construction Consumers (SLC3). She has spent more than twenty years in the AEC (Architecture, Engineering, and Construction) industry primarily serving in marketing/business development positions. Kelly earned her Bachelor of Art in Advertising, Marketing, and Media Communications with departmental honors from Webster University in St. Louis, Missouri. She also earned a Legal Studies Associates in Applied Science from St. Louis Community College–Meramec. She has spent twenty-seven years in marketing leadership roles and has been a speaker on many topics related to marketing communications. Prior to her current role, she owned a marketing, design, and web agency for eight years with many clients in the AEC industry and for many start-ups. She currently lives in Kirkwood, Missouri, with her husband of twenty-two years, Brad (an engineering manager), and is proud mom to their grown adopted daughter, Taylor.

314-278-8241
kjackson@slccc.net
www.linkedin.com/in/krjmarketing/

Jeanet Wade

Don't Grow it Alone

"Be smart, be safe, and remember the facts." I've heard those words on my way out the door for years. They usually come with a hug and a kiss, and they lift my heart and expand my thinking. Always. Everything I've grown into as an entrepreneur—a business leader, a consultant and coach, a best-selling author, and one of the first EOS Implementers™ to earn the designation of Expert—is directly linked to those words and to the person who still says them to me on a regular basis, my business partner and husband, Marshall.

In addition to this ritual, Marshall has encouraged and challenged me at every step of my journey. When I wrote *The Human Team: So, You Created A Team But People Showed Up!*, he contributed his wisdom and vision through writing and reviewing and encouraging me to go all in with promoting the book and the message of The 6 Facets of Human Needs™ and how they play into healthy teams and healthy business results.

"Be smart, be safe, and remember the facts" became part of our story of growth. We both knew that "be smart" meant so much more than intellect. It meant *use* your smarts, relate to people, be savvy, be you. And "be safe" meant be aware of your surroundings, be aware of others, be safe in relationships and in your environment. "Remember the facts" was Marshall's way of reminding me of my accomplishments and successes, in addition to the fact that, "People like you, they relate to you, you're capable of anything, and you're really good at what you do." These reminders helped me grow in confidence, and to be bold enough to try, to fail, and to try again and succeed.

Because of Marshall's unwavering and consistent involvement, I'm significantly better and more masterful at what I do each day. With his confidence and our connection, I've always known that I could give anything a shot and he'd be right there with me. Having that support professionally and personally has allowed me not only to grow in confidence but also to have the confidence to grow in so many other ways.

I haven't "grown it alone" out there in the world either. I've usually had people in my circle who supported my success, but my *growth* became exponential when I got clear on how I defined success and then surrounded myself with peers and professionals who held me to that definition and encouraged me to grow into it.

Most of us tend to define success by what our default circle says it means. However, the usual definitions of accomplishments, accolades, and acquisitions didn't create growth for me. Once I redefined success on my own terms, aiming instead for joy, abundance, and freedom, and surrounded myself with people who aligned with that definition, I was able to grow into the successes that followed.

To have joy, I learned to release and break through fear—both my fear of failure and my even bigger fear of success. One example was my experience with being named by *Small Business Monthly* as one of the "100 St. Louisans You Should Know to Succeed in Business." In addition to that recognition, they also put my picture on the cover of the magazine. I wanted to feel joy in that success, but I let some sniping and negative comments—which usually come with visible success—affect me too much. My fear of criticism and not being worthy enough was getting in the way of me feeling joy. That worry initially took a toll both emotionally and physically. I felt a significant weight to prove I was actually successful enough to deserve the award. I grew through the experience and realized that success isn't about the covers, the awards, or the accolades. I turned to different people for various consideration and support, such as sharing in my joy, healing physically, and helping me tap into the power of my mind. Within a short period of time, I found my way to feeling joy for my success.

It was much the same with abundance and freedom. To experience abundance, I had to let go of the idea that the only abundance that mattered—at least in professional success—was money. To experience freedom, I had to let go of the idea that I only got credit for success if I was in complete control and did everything myself. In addition, through the connection, consideration, and contribution of other people, I was able to grow into my own definition of success.

Today I have coaches, colleagues, mentors, and mentees who help me clarify, articulate, and create my purpose to share with the world. With them I have grown and better learned to love the challenges that allow me to continuously improve, develop new skills, and practice those skills on a journey toward mastery. I also belong to a peer advisory group that shares in my journey to be my best, and I have expert resources and business partners who help me focus my energy on what I do best. This all helps me to focus my time and makes it possible for me to raise myself to my highest best use while helping others do the same. This has allowed me to grow into the joy, abundance, and freedom that I need to be truly successful on my terms.

The other group of people who opened the door to tremendous growth is all of you. If you're reading this, you're part of the reason I'm continuing to grow. Growing requires giving. And giving requires someone who is there to receive. I've grown by giving my words, ideas, passions, expertise, time, and energy to others because, in that giving, I'm challenged to create more value to give. I've also grown by receiving because I'm fulfilled and rewarded when people who have received from me are willing, even eager, to reciprocate and add to my growth.

My story is really a story about humanity and how we grow. Not only do we not need to "grow it alone," the truth is we are usually better off including others. Growing into our potential, or "self-actualization," is a team activity. I've built my own human team: my husband and business partner, my coaches, peers, service providers, friends, colleagues, mentors, clients, audience members, and protégées. They have all contributed to my growth just as I have contributed to theirs.

Self-actualization, which is really just growth to a significant degree, happens only when our human needs are met. I call this framework The 6 Facets of Human Needs™, or sometimes "the 6 Cs" because each of them starts with a C: Clarity, Connection, Contribution, Consideration, Challenge, and Confidence. You may have noticed that these words run through every part of this story.

As I reflect on the individuals who have been part of my own growth, I can see how my "human team" has fulfilled all six of those needs for me. I've grown in Clarity of purpose, self-worth, and personal values. I've grown in my sense of Connection to myself, others, and the ideals I serve. I've grown in my ability to allow Contribution from others as well as my ability to contribute more meaningfully to them and to what matters to me. I've grown through giving Consideration to others and through receiving it as well. I've grown in my ability to Challenge and be challenged in healthy and exciting ways. Finally, I've grown in Confidence in my ideas, my talents, and my worth to the world.

By practicing "don't grow it alone," I have experienced the deepest, most significant success I could ask for: the feeling of having created joy, abundance, and freedom for myself and others by being part of a team of human beings who are growing together.

Jeanet Wade's focus is always on building healthy teams and healthy bottom lines. As the first Expert EOS Implementer™ in the St. Louis region, facilitating, teaching, and coaching the Entrepreneurial Operating System® (EOS®) to leadership teams at privately held companies, she developed a reputation for helping clients get Traction® on their Vision by leveraging her experience in marketing, innovation, and management. Because of her passion for people and her insights into the basic human needs that must be met in order to fully actualize the potential of a team, she quickly became known as *the* go-to resource for how to have effective, healthy teams that allow an organization to harness their people energy and maximize their "Return on Individual." She was named one of the "100 St. Louisans You Should Know to Succeed in Business" by *St. Louis Small Business Monthly*. Additionally, Jeanet is a featured ForbesBooks Author for her best-selling breakthrough book, *The Human Team: So, You Created A Team But People Showed Up!*

www.Business-Alchemist.com
www.linkedin.com/in/jeanet-wade-ab5500

Jamie Weaver

Growth is Change

Do you remember being in high school knowing that you were going to have to do something to pay your bills when you grew up? Some people were lucky enough to know what they wanted to be at a young age. Not me. My only goal was to afford a well-decorated, one-bedroom efficiency apartment, utilities, and my lifestyle.

It did not take long to realize that other people were making far more money and working half the hours I was working. The difference was that they had a certified skill or a degree. Soon after this discovery, I overheard an expert on a late-night informercial asking people to imagine the life they wanted to live. He instructed them to work backward from that picture. What do you need to start doing today to reach your goals? It amazes me how the right information comes to us when we are ready to hear it.

I needed a targeted plan for growth. Not just to grow older earning a paycheck, but to grow in a direction that I chose.

I decided to pursue my degree in Welding Technologies from our local community college. My father is a welder. I was one of the few female students in the program at the time. It was not easy to prove that I belonged there. I had one instructor who insisted on telling me daily that I was not going to smile my way through life. He challenged me to be a great student and learn everything the instructors were willing to teach. I did earn my welding degree, and three welding certificates too. Twenty-plus years later, people tell me that one of my best qualities is always having a smile.

It was a wonderful feeling to have successfully finished my degree… for a minute. Now I was going to have to find a job with someone who was willing to hire a woman welder. I applied everywhere in the region that I knew had welders on staff. I applied weekly at the places that had signs out front that said, "Now Hiring Welders." At that point in my life, I didn't realize they were not hiring me because I was a woman. One company told me my physical revealed that I had gallstones, and another said I did not pass the drug test. I honestly thought, "Maybe I do have gallstones? Maybe it was the little seeds on my hamburger buns that threw off my drug test?" Regardless. I persisted and eventually got two job offers! I had a choice about which job to accept. I chose the industrial job working as a pipe fitter.

Then a position opened at a steel distributor to sell pipe and tubing nationwide, and I got the job. My schooling and experience as a pipe fitter had given me the knowledge of the steel properties and an understanding of working with the materials. My coworkers were career account managers with a ton of knowledge they shared with me. I learned how to create a successful book of business from nothing, how to grow that book every year without putting myself at risk, and the importance of listening and being a friend.

It would be lovely if I could tell you that win was my happily ever after. But we are always growing, and each day we face new challenges as a result.

The next chapter of my life included being swept off my feet and married to my husband. We chose to start a family. This is not an abnormal thing to do, but it can be chaos for a woman's career. We both planned to continue working and chasing our career goals. Our newborn was in day care twelve hours a day. We were exhausted. We were broke. Day care is expensive. My husband was offered a promotion that meant he would need to travel 50 percent of the time. We decided he should take the job. He now made enough to cover our expenses. Together, we decided having extra money was not worth leaving our baby in day care all day and never having the time to see each other. We made the decision that I would resign and stay home with the children while he pursued his career. This sounds lovely, and it was. Looking back, I am thankful he and I work together well as a team, and we slowed down to enjoy those years as a family. This was not a popular choice at the time. Friends and family questioned the logic of quitting a good job that I had worked hard to get. I am sure others questioned me staying home while he was out working. This was a point in my life where I had to look inward, be authentic, and understand that growth and success are personal. We get one life, and I am not going to live mine by popular vote.

It was not long till our daughters had grown a bit bigger. I found an opportunity to go back to work part time. It was a position that allowed me to be gone only a few hours a day and do some of the work from home while the kids were sleeping. The position paid a lot less, but it gave me the opportunity to grow my skills and earn some extra money to do fun things with my family.

Once I was clear on my personal morals, values, and goals, choosing the right opportunities became much easier. Now our girls are in college, and we are in the season where they need money, and we are working to retire eventually. I am back to full time and focused on growing my career.

When I returned to the corporate world, I accepted a position in the commercial real estate market. I met many of the building owners in the St. Louis region, learned their priorities, and presented for corporate boards. This could have been a great position; unfortunately, the company culture was not for me. I left on my one-year anniversary. I joined forces with an established union commercial roofing company that had never done marketing or client development. The construction world was changing from hard bid to a firm needing to be invited to bid. I jumped in with both feet. This was a phenomenal learning experience. I was able to learn the ins and outs of the construction industry, the value of a network and associations, how to work with different personality types, and all the functions of marketing.

This is where I found the problem I wanted to solve. The best marketed company and the companies that are best at their craft are rarely the same. My professional purpose is connecting clients to the best solutions and to the brightest minds in the built environment. I believe everyone should have access to the top solutions and talents. Having safe buildings and quality infrastructure makes a difference in everyone's lives.

I am now working as a Senior Client Development Specialist for Terracon Consultants, Inc. My firm assists with the design portion of bridges, highways, buildings, and more. Being my authentic self and following my personal path guided the experiences that brought me here. Each stage of my life and every job I held shaped me into the person I am today. I would not know my professional purpose or have the skills to perform my role without each of those experiences.

Finding your own path will require you to be your authentic self to attract the right people and the right opportunities. The right ones are the only ones that count. Be mindful that not everyone is the right fit for you. Let them go.

Over the years, I have learned that growth happens when we are too busy living to look for it. Growth is often glamourized, but it is hard. The truth is, you will have outgrown who you were and what you were doing and now you must grow into who you are and your new responsibilities. Give yourself a little grace.

It has helped me immensely to understand that the only thing that is consistent is change. Growth is change. Changes can be scary. The ability for things to change also offers us hope.

Remember to care for yourself. Women can do anything except pour from an empty cup. When women support each other, we can move mountains. We still have a lot of work to do to achieve equality in the workplace. Consider offering a hand up to other women while you are waiting for your turn by giving them a referral, nominating them for an award, or giving them a shout-out to your network. The good you put into the world will come back to you in unexpected ways.

Jamie Weaver is a Senior Client Development Specialist at Terracon, a national engineering firm. She has over twenty years of experience in business development with a focus in blue-collar industries.

Jamie holds as Associates of Applied Sciences in Welding Technologies from Southwestern Illinois College, a certificate in Urban IPM from Purdue University, several certifications from the Disney Institute, and many technical certificates.

She was a contributing author to Upward: Leadership Lessons for Women on the Rise.

Jamie has served on the board for the Associated General Contractors of Missouri and still serves on several committees. She has contributed to her firm by winning the AGC1st award for multiple years, helping them win their first Keystone Award, and winning the overall Specialty Contractor of the Year award for their specific division.

In her free time, Jamie enjoys spending time with her family and friends at their hobby farm in Southern Illinois.

www.linkedin.com/in/jamie-weaver-21bab3124/
www.facebook.com/jamie.weaver.18/

Maite Nogales

The Many Roles of a Woman

I believe that *growth* is within us. We are born and are growing into many roles in our lives. This is a given and a constant.

Some women identify their growth early on and build their lives upon it, which I admire and congratulate. We need more women who trust themselves and go for it.

Then there are women like me, who realized later in life that growth is not as intimidating as it sounds, and that I have had a lifetime of practice. I am learning now how to trust myself and trust in the process. Show my grit and believe I can do it.

I started my active growth journey three years ago. I wanted to take time for myself, work on my professional and personal development, and explore my potential. A professional coach helped me work on my career. I wrote about this journey in my chapter, "Life is a Journey, Enjoy the Ride" in the book *Owning Your G.R.I.T.*, which helped me realize that a person can do almost anything if they put their mind to it.

Why is my chapter titled, "The Many Roles of a Woman"?

Women have many different roles in their lives in which they must adjust and evolve. We are constantly learning and developing. Growth is a constant companion. It all starts with us coming into this world and being a daughter.

I am a daughter. I am an only child, who tried to convince her mom that this wasn't a good thing, because I so desperately wanted a sibling. This lasted until I was twelve, when I told her the time was up now. A strong-willed child. I found my way through school by being neutral and not belonging to any groups or cliques. I was Maite, the one who always went for what she wanted and protected the ones who got picked on. When I look back, I realize that my mom had a big influence on who I am. She saw early on what I had in me, and she had trust in me and supported me where she could and always told me to be independent. Both my parents gave me everything: love, encouragement, support, a loving home, and security. I had an amazing childhood, and growing up was easy. I was fortunate and privileged, and I thank my parents for that. Over the years, I grew into an independent woman with dreams, ambitions, and fears.

I am a wife. A partner, listener, supporter, facilitator, and lover. Suddenly you are adding all these roles to your repertoire, and you start discovering your growth together. I am fortunate to have found my husband, who supports and challenges me at the same time. I have learned this is an incredible gift to have found someone like him who asks the right questions, challenges my thinking, encourages me to try new things, and supports my new endeavors. Yes, we have arguments and disagreements, but we have found a way to compromise and find solutions. This is growth; it goes both ways. With growth comes appreciation in my world. If you have a person in your life who supports and lifts you up, show your appreciation to that person and don't forget to say it out loud.

I am a mom. Being a mom has been the greatest growth and change in my life. I always knew I wanted children, but little did I know that this would change my life entirely. My two children mean the world to me, but boy are they hard work. They can challenge me! They help me grow every day. They also love me no matter what, and that is a very soothing and calming feeling. I sometimes must stop and embrace that and remember I am trying my best as a mother. I push the guilty feelings away and try to live in the moment with my children. Kids are resilient, and they know you better than anybody else. If I can show my children my love and support, I am convinced they feel it!

Mothers have so many roles. Suddenly a woman becomes the caregiver, cook, housekeeper, playmate, educator, chauffeur—the family manager, really! I've learned what it's like to be responsible for this little individual who learns from and watches me. As mothers, we have the chance to show our children that growth is natural, exciting, and helpful for their future. Encourage them to go for it and to be whatever they want to be. It is hard work, but it pays off.

I am a colleague. In my role at work, there are expectations and goals, but there are also opportunities. I am evolving into and gaining the confidence of a leader. I won't lie—it is intimidating and scary at times. I want to grow, and with growth comes determination and hard work. When people are thriving under your leadership or are motivated to do more, your hard work is paying off. As I've grown, I've realized that being a leader was what I wanted to be all along. I really like it. I accelerate, feel energized, and love my role of empowering others.

I am a friend. I am caring, loud, determined, honest, and outgoing. That is how I see myself, but I wondered how others see me. I thought, why not ask people around me what their perspective is? So I asked fifty people, including friends, family, colleagues, neighbors, and teammates, the following question: "If you think about me, which three to five words come to mind?" It's very awkward to ask for that kind of feedback. I was amazed by the spontaneity and willingness to answer, and how quickly some responses came in. Some people asked if I got hacked or if the question was a trap. Others asked what I needed the information for or said that three to five words were not enough to describe me. The outcome was amazing.

(*To everyone who responded to my little survey, thank you. I truly appreciate your feedback. Not only was it an amazing experience filled with insight, but I also used the outcome to demonstrate how powerful your feedback was. You all helped me to grow even more, and you are part of my chapter!*)

Forty-six people responded and used seventy-five words to describe me, which is mind-blowing and humbling. Reading these words was so emotional and encouraging at the same time. Here are the top five words:

1. **Kind:** This word is very humbling. Who doesn't want to be kind?

2. **Determined:** I appreciate this word and wouldn't want to trade being determined for anything.

3. **Caring and Loving:** I am proud to hear that people think this way about me, as these are very important traits to me.

4. **Beautiful:** I hope this means inside and out, which is a beautiful thing to say about someone.

5. **Confident:** I don't always see myself this way, as I often question myself, overthink things, or am afraid to fail. I once read this very powerful sentence, "Leap and the net will appear." I am not a risk-taker yet, but I am working on it.

Feedback is precious; take it all in and learn from it. As I've matured, it's clearer to me what life has to offer. I can choose who I want to be, how I want to show up, how I want to continue to grow, and how to navigate complicated situations or decisions and learn from my mistakes. I am calmer, which helps me to see with more clarity, take my time, breathe, and let go.

Writing this chapter was a satisfying process because it invited me to take time to write and reflect on my achievements and think about my goals for the future. Women don't take enough time to reflect. While fulfilling all these roles as a woman, we are exhausted, tired, and it is easy to forget that we are also individuals who have needs, feelings, and thoughts.

Now it is time for *you*—yes you, my dear reader. I challenge you take the time and ask the people around you the three to five words that best describe you. Get ready to welcome this honest feedback, then embrace it.

In the end, we discover growth as an opportunity to move forward, to flourish, and as something to take advantage of instead of to fear. When we see it as *growth* and decide we have the grit to take it on and trust in ourselves, a whole new world opens—new opportunities that will catapult us to a new chapter of our lives. I strongly believe that we can change the narrative; we just have to believe it.

Maite Nogales is a networking specialist with twenty years of international professional experience in marketing and communications. She is part of the employee and community engagement team, managing the global volunteer program, Curiosity Labs™ at MilliporeSigma, the Life Science business of Merck KGaA in Darmstadt, Germany. Her goal is to inspire the next generation of scientists with hands-on experiments, to demonstrate the diversity of a science career, and to empower students to follow their dreams.

Maite is an international best-selling author of the anthology *Owning Your G.R.I.T.* and the cofounder of the C.A.R.E. (Change & Action for Racial Equity) initiative in St. Louis, whose vision is creating inclusive communities and offering opportunities to all regardless of race, creed, or social status.

Maite is a multicultural mother of two, who enjoys being active with family and friends. You can find her on the slopes skiing or on the courts playing tennis. She loves to read, watch a good movie, and also enjoys being a culinary chef.

www.linkedin.com/in/maite-nogales
www.facebook.com/maite.nogales.1
www.twitter.com/maite_nogales

Cassy Range

The Rescuer

Well, I did it! Since my previous chapter, published last year in Owning Your G.R.I.T., I graduated with my bachelor's degree and accomplished a huge life goal. I envisioned this goal for myself for many years, and it was everything I expected. After taking my last final exam, I burst into tears the moment I closed my laptop and immediately asked myself, "What next?"

Middle adulthood is often a time for great reflection and change. At this stage in life, approaching forty years old, I know I want more, so I have enrolled in graduate school to obtain my master's degree. I often think about how my childhood experiences shaped me as a person, my behaviors, self-esteem, and personality. I struggled a great deal from childhood until early adulthood with my mental health. I made a lot of bad choices as a young woman because I was lost and shame was attached to those choices. My trauma was chipping away at who I was, until I was left with no sense of self.

We all have trauma in some form. I have been thinking about those traumas and figuring out how I can overcome the feelings that come with those experiences and how I can use them in a positive way. We all take on a role in our families, and my role was rescuer and/or peacemaker. This has affected all my relationships because they were often built on me being some sort of enabler. As a young woman, I always wanted to "fix" everything. I wanted to repair relationships, help others who were struggling, and make everyone happy, but this created a personality of perfectionism and put loads of pressure on me to be responsible at a very young age.

This role is a huge part of who I am today. My business was built around being a problem-solver for my clients. I often offer to fix problems for family, friends, and anyone I see who is struggling. I am extremely empathetic, which has been a great tool in life. I am a great listener and communicator. This behavior has brought me remarkable success in business, but it has also brought me years of anxiety and depression. For a long time, I was lost and scared on the inside, but on the outside I seemed strong, ambitious, and seemed happy to everyone around me. In my mind, weakness was not an option, and I would only show the parts of myself that could be useful to others. I had to be strong for everyone around me, to my own detriment.

I was lucky enough to grow up with parents who instilled in me the values of hard work, kindness, and to always finish what you start. I have had great mentors in life as well, mostly business owners whom I worked for and family members who really saw me and guided me along the way. My parents built a resilience in me, from watching them overcome their own battles and never giving up. I have had a couple great bosses as well, who gave me a chance and saw something in me that I didn't see yet in myself, which helped to build my confidence.

To be our best selves in life, we need to understand who we are and what we want. This is often a puzzling question for people, and can even be frightening to answer because we do not know. Most of my life, I have been so focused on my family and career that I have not taken much time for myself. In the process, I never took the time to ask myself these same questions. Recently, with my desire to work on myself and manifesting my best life, I am on a new journey into understanding who I am and what I want.

Understanding how our childhood and youth has shaped us, what roles we have taken, and how we approach situations is a great start to accomplishing growth and resilience. For me, understanding why I behave the way I do in certain situations has allowed me to stop and sit in my feelings before reacting. I can become incredibly defensive when I feel like my work product or integrity is being questioned, and this comes from being a perfectionist and not ever wanting to disappoint anyone. I will often react immediately when someone needs help, not stopping to think why I feel such a need to rescue. I understand now that I do not want to feel the guilt of not helping, so I often help, but out of selfish reasons.

When we take on a role in life, our brains are so wired to react within that role that it takes such a significant effort to break those habits. This is the work that needs to be done to accomplish self-growth. It is difficult for me to not offer help, or to say no, and when I do I must sit in that feeling of guilt. That is where the change happens—sitting in those feelings and letting them pass. When we're aware of our feelings like this, we start to build the mindfulness of what we desire in life. This leads to the change we want and need to fully know who we are.

To grow into the woman I want to be, I have made an earnest effort to set goals for myself, practice mindfulness and motivation, and using my time wisely on my priorities each day. I want to use my empathetic and hardworking nature to be successful in all areas of life. My path was not easy, and we all have experiences in life that can chip away at who we really are and what we want, but if we take a step back and look at those behaviors and how we can change and grow into the women we want to be, it is powerful. It can be difficult to not get stuck in feelings of despair, resentment, and sadness when we think about life's struggles and traumas, but it is possible to change and use those experiences to fully understand how we are built and to see the beautiful lessons that come from challenging times in life.

I often take action to keep myself motivated, like telling the world I was getting my bachelor's degree in my last book. That was a very vulnerable moment. I didn't know how I would be judged for not already being a college graduate, and I wondered if I failed, how embarrassed I would feel. Strategically, it motivated me more to finish what I started, and freed me to be fully honest about who I am. This step created motivation and change and helped me let go of any shame I have held onto over the years. Just like saying no to people when I do not really want to do something, telling the world about my challenges and goals and owning who I am are all steps to my best life.

So many self-help books, social media posts, and information is out there about living your best life. Of course, taking steps like breaking unhealthy habits, setting goals, and using your time wisely are all great plans for a better life. I believe, though, that if you do not dig deeply into who you really are and see how life has shaped you as a person and what you really want, you won't ever achieve complete happiness. It is also important to be mindful about how you are evolving and changing and what that means for your desires in life. In ten years, twenty years, my aspirations and nature will have changed and evolved, and I need to constantly check in with myself and what that looks like.

Above all, mental health is something that needs to be nurtured and strengthened in order for us to fully develop into our best selves. Over the last ten years, I have been happy to see more advocacy for mental health in the counseling profession and how the social perspective has changed immensely. If you are struggling in any way, I strongly recommend getting help from a mental health professional. A great deal of my growth has happened through talking with a professional who created the space for me to be completely honest and vulnerable when I needed it. These counselors gave me the tools to make the changes I needed after spending many years feeling depressed and anxious.

I have two young sons and a loving husband who have motivated me to make a change and to be the best version of myself, to believe in myself, and to set the best example I can. For that, I want to say thank you to them and dedicate this chapter to my two joys in life, Daxten and Hudson.

Cassy Range is the founder of Range Professional Services, LLC, an accounting and business management firm. She is also a proud mother of two young boys, Dax and Hudson. Range Professional Services offers remote full-service accounting, office administration, and consulting for small- to medium-sized businesses. Cassy launched her business in 2013 after working in the field of accounting and business management for over ten years. Her combined experience covers all aspects of business, which helps her clients utilize one company for many needs. Cassy has worked in various industries including health care, food and beverage, retail, construction, and real estate, and she is highly trained in law firm accounting and management. Along with her husband, Chad Range, Cassy launched a law firm investigation company in 2020, Range Investigation Services, LLC. She is currently working on new business ideas, so stay tuned!

cassy@rangeproservices.com
www.rangeproservices.com/
www.rangeinvestigation.com/

Monica Bailey

Saved for DE&I

If I had the chance to talk to a younger me about my life and experiences, there are just a few things that I would change. One, I would have had my grandmother in my life for more than twenty years. This is because she was my savior (truly). Granny, as we lovingly called her, rescued my older brother and me from a drug-addicted single mom in San Francisco in the early 1970s. As young children (about six and eight), my brother and I did not know how bad the situation was, but our Granny did. Growing up, I did not have a certain dream or aspiration of what I wanted to be or who I was destined to become. Some children know early on exactly what it is that want to be when they grow up. I did not have a clue, and I didn't really think of myself as a "savior of sorts" at any age, not even when I became an adult.

I began in the workplace at the young age of sixteen years through a high school co-op intern program. I remember the interviews (I was a nervous wreck) with women who were not much older and became like older sisters. We are still the best of friends today. They welcomed and even helped me with transportation, picking me up from half-day class at my high school. I wore my cheerleading uniform to the office on game days. The job was as a summer file clerk in the operations department in the construction industry. I worked hard and proved myself, so there were permanent job opportunities offered. I accepted a full-time position that became available that fall (1983) and worked in several departments and for several different people over the years. My heart and passion were always on wanting more for others and helping in whatever way possible.

My grandmother taught me many things. One was that God cares for me, and that I should look and pray to him for *all* things in my life. That meant being a loving, caring, and kind person, and always giving back, knowing someone's situation may be worse than mine. I've always lived my life with these values in mind.

I had many examples in my company and the industry of others I could look to and look up to for guidance. Little did I realize, I was being raised by my workplace family, because I lost my grandmother and mother in the late 80's. Many of my "work family" members helped guide and mold me. Their care started me on my growth journey. I watched, listened, and learned everything I could while observing my coworkers and colleagues. All the while, I was still trying to figure out who I was to become.

Being a Black female in a large construction firm in the early 80s was a rarity. I could count on one hand how many coworkers and colleagues looked like me. I thought I was a unique person, but later it struck me as odd. The more I explored different career opportunities at my company, the more I realized how diversity was lacking in our industry. I thought, "Where are the people who look like me? Where are the minority-owned firms that want to do business with this amazing company I work for?"

"If we're already considered a successful company," the thought was, "is there more work we can do in this area?" Facing that question is the first step to real change.

That is exactly what happened around 2004, when my regional president posed the question about our current DE&I efforts. "This is an area that you're passionate about, Monica?" my boss asked. "Absolutely!" I responded. He took a leap of faith in me, and so did I. At this point in my career, I realized my calling was DEI: Diversity, Equity, and Inclusion. The term was not used much in the early 2000s, especially in the construction industry. Most of our industry looked at diversity as a mandate, more of a "Check the Box" requirement. What we wanted to do was change the narrative when it came to DEI. This meant being proactive versus reactive—starting with establishing internal policies and procedures and leadership that backs you all the way. That seems positive and easy, right? Well, let me tell you, it wasn't then, and it still isn't easy now in 2022. It's just not as simple as it sounds. You must be very intentional, and hope that cultural and emotional intelligence kicks in at some point.

The title of this book resonates with my entire DE&I journey. *GROWTH* equals:

Giving

Resilience

Opportunities

Willingness

Time

Helping

Without this mindset, all our DEI efforts will fail. There must be a mutual understanding of all parties involved (including clients, our owners, consumers of construction, general contractors, prime subs, first-tier subs working directly for general contractors, and MWBE (Minority & Women Owned Businesses) firms. To succeed we all must work toward the same common goal. I put every ounce of energy into trying to convince others that it's just the right thing to do. Seems easy, right? Wrong. What I noticed was that people who were passionate and positive about being proactive did not have to be convinced; they just did it and led by example. Throughout the years, I saw positive changes. More minority- and woman-owned businesses began working on more projects in our region, and more people of color and women filled open professional and craft positions in our industry. But was it enough?

I have many great friends and colleagues in the industry who are passionate about this work and are working incredibly hard to improve this effort. Diversity professionals have a common goal—we want our partners and firms to succeed. If they are successful, we all are! DEI professionals are constantly sharing information with each other, not looking at it as competitive or secretive, but asking the question, "How can we help?" Finally, it's starting to resonate that if we as an industry want to prosper, we better get in front of the ball, not behind it (proactive vs. reactive). We must have diverse opinions and representation to help us grow, survive, and be relevant in the future.

As a result of this journey, one of the things that I would tell my younger self now is that resilience and patience are virtues in the DEI race. To effect change, these two virtues must be top of mind. I have hit many walls in my career, and have had many doors closed, but a positive attitude and persistence go a long way. I worked hard to "make it make sense." I stayed steadfast and optimistic that "I" was going to make a difference, and at the end of the day, I feel like I did (even if it was small).

"The "needle has moved," but resilience and patience go a long way. If you're representing a minority- or woman-owned business, you must ask, "How long do I have to wait to get an opportunity? I've put in the work, I've established my business; why am I always second, third, or even last?" I've listened to many stories from people throughout my thirty-eight years in the industry, specifically the minority community. Just like any person in any business that we encounter, we share the same moral values. All we want is a fair chance to do business with you, to work at and with large businesses, to be mentored by experienced, successful people—*not* because I am a minority business or person, but because *I'm great at what I do*!

I would say at the end of my career, I am satisfied with "moving the needle," and that I am very hopeful that in another five to ten years we will not be having these same conversations, but instead we will be hearing many more stories of success in companies that I worked with in our community. One day in the not so distant future, we won't have to rely on diversity directors at corporations, making sure "we" are checking a box; there will be corporations hiring diversity professionals to help guide and drive policy to make sure that we are all being culturally competent in our everyday thinking in our personal and professional lives.

I now have two adult daughters, and I've tried to lead by example of the things I've learned throughout my life and career. They never got to meet my granny, but they know who she was and what she meant to me. I had to grow up very fast and be independent at early age in life. Hopefully, I've passed on positive traits to be successful growing up and leading by example to others. As I did, I hope they have some of the same positive influences and experiences throughout their journey in life.

So, in closing, circling back to my savior (my granny), I guess I was saved from my situation to make something of myself and to make a difference in others' lives throughout my life's journey and career.

"She is clothed with *strength* and *dignity,* and she *laughs* without fear of the future." – Proverbs 31:25 (NLT)

Monica Bailey retired in 2021 after spending her entire thirty-eight-year career at McCarthy Building Companies. She served as Director of Diversity for McCarthy's thirty-state central region, facilitating effective diversity, equity, and inclusion practices between the firm's project staff and the business community. She has successfully impacted dozens of projects throughout the region—from the Washington University Campus Transformation project and the St. Louis Union Station Aquarium, to the National Geospatial-Intelligence Agency (NGA), to name a few.

Monica served on the diversity task force of the Associated General Contractors of Missouri and the Associated General Contractors of America National Diversity Steering Council, the diversity committee of the St. Louis Council of Construction Consumers, and on the boards of directors for the St. Louis Construction Forum and the Regional Union Construction Center. A 2016 graduate of the Coro™ Women in Leadership Program, sponsored by Focus St. Louis, she volunteers in the Mentor St. Louis program of the Boys & Girls Clubs of Greater St. Louis.

Monica was honored as Diversity Champion by *St. Louis Small Business Monthly* in 2014, received the Diverse Business Leader Award from the *St. Louis Business Journal* in 2017, and was named Inclusion Champion for St. Louis Council of Construction Consumers in 2020.

Born and raised in St. Louis, Monica is married with two daughters.
Mbbizsolutions@gmail.com
www.linkedin.com/in/monica-bailey-280bb556
www.facebook.com/monica.bailey.792
twitter.com/monicaB76901305

Lynda J. Roth

Growing with the Digital Age

"Don't go through life, grow through life."
– Eric Butterworth

For me, growth has been a lifelong adventure. I was born and raised in the mid-twentieth century when the USA had entered an era of relative peace and meteoric growth. During my childhood, the USA built the space industry and landed a man on the moon in less than ten years after President Kennedy's address. Also during that time, the Information Technology industry came of age. When I graduated from high school, I had no idea what I wanted to do as an adult. What I did know was that I wanted to have a career, not just a job. I met with my high school counselor, who suggested I enroll in the new computer science curriculum at the community college. He promised me I would start my career in two years. I had no idea what it was, but it sounded perfect, so I enrolled.

On the first day of class when the instructor demonstrated wire board programming, I questioned my sanity, but my dad encouraged me to stick it out. I am so grateful I followed his advice. To my surprise, much of the curriculum came easily to me. I never had to program a wire board, but I graduated third in my class. Based on that placement, the head of the department helped me obtain a great job at Ralston Purina where I grew tremendously in knowledge and confidence. Next, I had an opportunity to work for Levi Strauss. That turned into a great growth opportunity, where I worked on advanced technology projects and moved to California.

Over the next ten years, my knowledge and opportunities grew along with the industry. I had a major career and personal growth spurt when I identified a key business need for corporate executives to have high-level business information. I decided to start and build a software company to fill that need. Sounded like a great idea; now the question was "How?"

First, I needed to recruit a team. I built a team consisting of a few great software developers and database designers. Our small group worked to design the system in our free time. With a good design, we were able to engage our first client—a group of hospitals. They were looking for key metrics regarding patient services profitability. With our design, we developed the system they needed. This was a significant advanced financial information system that could now be sold to other clients.

The next opportunity was with a major bank in Los Angeles. They were already working on a system but weren't making much progress. When we demonstrated our product, they were thrilled, and we were quickly hired to build the system for them. We made the same deal that we would retain ownership of the generic system when completed. My goal from this project was to finish with a completed generic system that we could package and start selling as a product. This turned out to be a bigger challenge than I expected, which resulted in significant growth for me.

I was responsible for managing the entire project, the bank's team, and my team, and coordinating with the primary consulting firm. Finally, I also had to design all the functionality in the system and code some of it. With a significant amount of work over a year and half, the project was a major success. The bank executives were very happy and agreed to a long-term maintenance contract. Most importantly, we had a system that could now be sold as a software product! Not only was it a period of tremendous personal growth both in my profession and in my interpersonal skills, but it was also a major step forward for our fledgling company.

During the next few years, we hired a professional sales representative, partnered with the database software company we used in the system, and landed marquee clients including American Express. My experience starting and growing a software company was a major growth experience for me.

With all our progress, I felt we were on our way. In the early nineties, technology infrastructure shifted from mainframe computers to client server architecture. We were going to need to redesign the system on the new technology platforms. The technology industry was changing rapidly, our database partner went bankrupt, and we needed to address the changes. Once again, funding was a top priority. I negotiated a deal with a software vendor to purchase the rights to our system for use in the banking industry. I met with my partners to discuss how to move forward. Instead of redesigning the system, they voted to use the funds to continue to sell to the mainframe market. I realized that was not a winning strategy and left my company. Within a year my partners were bankrupt. So now I was poised to grow again by starting my management consulting practice.

For the next twenty years, I worked with major corporations and mid-market companies to transform them to new technology platforms. Each of those projects was a growth opportunity, and I had a very fulfilling career.

While I enjoyed my clients and the transformations we achieved, my life was changing. I was rapidly nearing the magic age of sixty-five. Each of those projects required years to complete, and I didn't want to keep spending my life doing them. My parents had passed, my nieces and nephews were grown and were marrying and starting families. I decided it was time for a major life change that would start with a move back to Missouri to be close to family and lifelong friends.

Even though I was reaching retirement age, I had absolutely no interest in retiring. The information technology industry was more important and relevant than ever, and I had the greatest growth opportunity since college. With over forty years of experience transforming companies with new technologies, I was poised to design an entire second career and life for myself. For the first time, I was going to step back and design my own life.

However, I had no experience and no idea how to do this! First, I believed I had a lot to say. Digital technology was changing society and business. Businesses that did not embrace digital technology would not survive. So the first step in my new life was to become an author. Contrary to what I expected, it was not a solitary experience.

I spent a year researching and writing my book and then another several months editing, rewriting, and obtaining reviews. I collaborated with a business associate who was the transformational CEO for KBB (Kelly Blue Book) in the nineties. He provided me with the KBB story, helped edit the book's content, and contributed the book foreword. I also interviewed other business executives and directors to obtain their perspectives. Writing a book was challenging, fun, collaborative, and introspective. It did not result in much revenue, however.

The next decision in my life design involved determining how to generate revenue, how much free time I wanted, and what I really wanted to do that would be both valuable to clients and enriching for me. I still feel like I have a lot to say. I want to share my knowledge and experience with others through speaking, teaching, and coaching. To do that, I have become a professional speaker, author, executive consultant, and corporate board member. In the digital technology era, you must be noticed on social media. LinkedIn is where my prospects are, so I have begun taking advantage of that platform to post information, grow my network, and build relationships. I have already received an offer to teach a virtual class to executives in Malaysia on Digital Transformation. I authored a chapter in *Owning Your G.R.I.T.* and contributed this *Growth* chapter. I contracted with a team to guide me in starting a podcast on digital transformation, and I am contemplating a sequel to my first book.

The fun part of this phase of my life is I get to enjoy my Corvette, see the country instead of just fly over it, and spend time with family and friends. I took a five-day trip with my Corvette Club last summer and hope to do another soon. I have been taking time to be with friends and family. I visited my sisters in Arizona over Christmas and have spent time with my dearest cousin in the last few years. I was on the committee for my 50th high school reunion and enjoyed being close to lifelong friends and planning a spectacular reunion. It was a very memorable evening.

Since I made this change in my life, I have been more excited about life and more fulfilled than I have in years. In the words of George Eliot, female nineteenth-century author of *Silas Marner*:

"It is never too late to be who you might have been."

Lynda J. Roth is the author of *Digital Transformation: An Executive Guide to Survive and Thrive in the New Economy,* and for decades has been transforming businesses to become more productive, profitable, and relevant. In today's rapidly changing digital world, business transformation has become more critical.

Lynda is passionate about guiding executives of traditional businesses through a transition to a business that will survive and thrive in the digital age.

Lynda worked in her father's HVAC business as a teenager. She loved business and developed a keen eye for business operations. She studied information technology and business finance in college and started her career in technology. She has managed multimillion-dollar technology transformation projects, started and grown her own software firm, and successfully transformed her client companies to compete in the digital world.

www.linkedin.com/in/lyndajroth/
lynda@ljrcs.com
818-216-7264
www.ljrconsultingservices.com

Heather Torretta

Create, Learn, Think

There are times in your life where you feel "less than." Those times rob you of confidence and happiness. Those times can also make you push yourself to learn more and eventually be better. Sometimes the negative hangs around longer than you prefer before you get to the positive. Other times the two get mixed together. Being a part of *Owning Your G.R.I.T.*, the first book in this anthology series, was an example of this mixture of positive and negative for me. I am a voracious reader of many genres and thought it would be great to write and publish a book one day. When the opportunity came up to be a part of *Owning Your G.R.I.T.*, I said yes to the opportunity.

Positive thoughts about the project came first: the great adventure, all the exposure, meeting new people, being a published author, and so many other good feelings. My second thoughts were more negative. One was a lack of confidence about being a writer. I love to read, so why would writing be difficult? When I read, I edit without realizing it and opt to not read authors with poor spelling and grammar. Then, my next negative thought was annoyance with myself for agreeing to write a chapter. What was I thinking? I knew nothing about book publishing. What if I discovered I was a horrible writer? Would that ruin my reading hobby? It was incredibly uncomfortable, and I didn't like that I had gotten myself into the mess. But I gave my word, so write I must.

Later I discovered how much help the team would provide. Jen Bardot found a company to publish, edit, and help promote our book. The team was amazing. After I spoke with them and some of the other authors about their chapters, it came to me: the book was a great idea, but contributing a chapter meant I needed to write about my personal life and not just the parts where I look good. As a private person, it was difficult to speak, let alone write, a chapter about my life. What was even more daunting was squishing over a decade of my life into the pages of that chapter. It took hours, tears, and lots of scowling at the screen, but I got a first draft done.

Fast-forward a couple of weeks, and I attended the meetings and meet-and-greets with the other authors. There were forty authors total, plus the publishing team. At first, networking with them was uncomfortable. The social awkwardness of the pandemic made sure of that, but it wasn't as difficult as I had feared. I relaxed after spending some time with several of the ladies and listening to their stories. I still hadn't written my chapter, but at least I was having fun.

Even before the pandemic, attending events exhausted me. All the people, small talk, and posturing meant that it would take me a couple of days to get back to my normal. I can do it, but I don't look forward to it. Add in the pandemic stress, and I was even more tired. Yet being with the other authors taught me that it depends on who I am surrounded by at an event. There are certain types of people who take energy and certain types that give it. It's important to be around enough people who make you comfortable and happy so that you are trading energy with each other. I look back at past networking events and see this to be true. It doesn't mean that I'm not exhausted by the end of the day; rather, it means I am having more fun.

After I attend an event now, I give myself a three-minute freewriting session where I jot down all my thoughts on the event as they pop into my head. Words, sentences, phrases, all of it. Then I sort out the positive and negative. I write about what I can do differently at the next event. Finally, I evaluate whether it was worth attending the event and if I will go to others like it. For events that I must attend, I come prepared with a clear plan and leave once I have completed it. The plan is what's best for me as a person. I do push myself a bit each time, but I know there are limits. I am a fierce enforcer of them now.

Another event I was not dreading but wasn't looking forward to either was the launch party. I had met a couple of the other women, but not most of them. My husband and kids came with me to cheer me on. My kids spent the night asking the other authors for autographs and talking about being an author. It meant a lot to me to have them there. My family is an important part of my life, and everyone had fun.

The first draft of my chapter was horrible. There were misspellings, run-on sentences, and grammatical errors everywhere. I mixed past and present tense, sometimes in the same sentence. There were errors that I knew were incorrect but couldn't and didn't bother naming what they were. They just needed to be fixed somehow. It was embarrassing how bad the first draft was. It was also liberating to have it done! It was not ready to publish by any means, but the first draft was complete and ready to be edited. My final chapter would come about seven drafts later. I kept reminding myself this was a marathon, not a sprint.

Through the process, I discovered that my writing style does not work well by sitting in front of a screen, waiting for inspiration. That blank page does not speak to me. It blocks my creativity, and what is written doesn't sound like me. I am not an annotated outline, follow-the-plan type of writer. I have thoughts that I want to convey, and I write them down as they pop into my head. At a certain point (and many notes later), I feel confident to start writing, but not before that. Even then, I may still trash my first or second rough drafts.

The book launch was something of a blur as there were so many people promoting the book. Social media is a powerful force. I posted a little for the book but didn't have many people following me. I didn't feel comfortable posting in general. Now, I have learned that it's best for me to remember that the people I connect with on social media want to see me succeeding and happy. I also met with a gentleman who made social media click for me. With his help, and after reading books, blogs, and opinions on the best way to have a presence online, I found my way. My social media plan is easy to visualize in my head, takes little time once I learn what I am doing, and is easily repeatable. My social media videos aren't perfectly edited, with on-point lighting or high resolution, but I'm creating and sharing them. Each week I work on improving one thing for my next video. I try to learn new skills, such as creating memes to post. It's a slow and long road, and I may never be an expert, but I am doing it.

Even a well-thought-out plan will have obstacles, detours, and road-blocks. My plan for being a part of *Owning Your G.R.I.T.* was like that. There were times when I wasn't sure whether to continue on the path or change course. I took detours that dead-ended quickly, while others took a while before they ended. The best detours led me back to the main path. Some detours were much harder to get through than others, while a couple that seemed large ended up being quite easy to work through. The point is, I had the option of saying I didn't want to be a part of the book, but instead I said yes.

I still talk with several of the other authors regularly, as we have so much in common. I now understand the steps of book publishing and can visualize my plan if I decide to write my own book. I have a process I use when I attend events to recover more quickly from them. My presence on social media is better than it used to be and will be a little better each week going forward.

There are times in life where you feel "less than," but if you take them as opportunities to learn, you can feel more than you ever thought. Create. Learn. Think. You will find your happiness in the obstacle course that is life.

Heather Torretta is an avid reader, traveler, mother, wife, entrepreneur, volunteer, salsa dancer, and lifelong learner. She is a contributing author in *Owning Your G.R.I.T.* Her company Prevailing Wage Consulting, LLC educates companies on the labor compliance reporting requirements on prevailing wage and Davis-Bacon Act projects. She graduated from the University of Missouri–St. Louis with a couple of bachelor's degrees: Accounting, Business Administration, and Criminology & Criminal Justice. Her background in accounting with an emphasis in small business has helped Heather assist many small businesses over the years. She is the leader of an amazing Girl Scout troop, captain to an all-girl robotics team, leader to an amazing den of Cub Scouts, and spends as much time with her family as possible. She believes life is often quite serious, so laugh and listen more as the happiness is usually right around the corner.

linkedin.com/in/heather-torretta-69035251
www.facebook.com/heather.torretta
heathermtorretta@gmail.com

Melissa Grizzle

No Bandwidth for Personal Growth Today

When asked to contribute to this anthology, my gut reaction was to say no, mainly because it scared me. The irony of turning down the opportunity to grow through writing about my relationship with growth was obvious to me as well. Fortunately, I am a fan of situations with a strong "meta" component, so I decided to let that attraction win out and said yes to this adventure.

I soon found myself staring at a blank screen, struggling where to begin, cursing my backyard garden whose new spring growth was supposed to inspire and was failing right out of the gate. Weeks of contemplation on my ideal approach for this deconstruction of growth still felt insufficient and uncertain, but acknowledging that feeling was in fact the perfect place to start. I have a strong yet unrealistic desire to not only be immediately skilled at whatever I try, and recognized for it, but also to be clear on my path ahead. These aspects of my personality have probably influenced my growth journey more than any others. And it doesn't take a genius to see how these unrealistic expectations could significantly limit one's possibilities for growth.

The concept that to be good at something you must be willing to be bad at it first makes sense in my head. But it often feels paralyzing to the rest of my body. It takes courage to dive into something knowing you are going to initially suck. I often wish I was more innately wired to just jump in and try, or able to muster the courage to face the intense mental and physical discomfort I naturally feel. My quest to find a way to lessen those discomforts while not revealing my shortcomings has been an ongoing challenge when it comes to capitalizing on opportunities to grow.

This deeper exploration of my relationship with growth has allowed me to develop a greater appreciation for the interconnectedness of our key personality traits. I've realized the pride I take in being keenly self-aware adds a layer of complexity. Not only do I have the need to be knowledge-able or skilled from the get-go, but in the rare moments I'm not, I must then know that about myself and be the first to acknowledge it. Fighting the urge to explain and defend myself is a tendency I struggle with on a regular basis.

If you've read my bio, you may be wondering how someone so uncomfortable with failing has spent almost twenty years working with entrepreneurs. Well, it turns out that when one lives at the center of the Venn diagram of constantly striving for perfection, seeking external validation and admiration, and wanting to be a champion for growth (with as little hypocrisy as possible), the innovation community is a great environment in which to work on resolving that tension. I am reminded regularly how contagious mindsets and behaviors can be and have chosen to consistently expose myself to those I want to emulate. If you hang out with risk-taking, courageous innovators long enough, you begin to act like them.

I am also regularly reminded how quickly we can miss growth opportunities when relying too heavily on what we already know about ourselves. When it comes to our personal growth journeys, these inaccurate assumptions can result in rejecting something that could be a perfect match, or at least a valuable experience if we lean into it. As my husband pointedly responded when I expressed surprise that we never crossed paths on Match.com, "Look me in the eye and tell me you ever searched for 'some college' (one of the filters for education level)." He was right; a college degree was a must for this daughter of academicians, a fourth generation of college-educated women. I had filtered out the power of possibility created by deviating from that belief.

I will refrain from further exploration of the myriad ways my husband and I differ, and how my life is better for it. For now, I will just say this: find people to share your life who can both foster your growth and be a soft place to land—and who aren't offended when you invoke the "I don't have the bandwidth for personal growth today!" out-clause and escape to go weed your garden alone.

Returning to my professional world, I have the fortunate role known as an "innovation ecosystem builder" where I help mold the environment to be a catalyst for innovation and entrepreneurship. I also experience its impact on my own growth every day. As Austin Kleon reminds us in his book, *Steal Like an Artist: 10 Things Nobody Told You About Being Creative*, we are "a mashup of what [we] choose to let into [our] lives." Surrounding myself with people who have personal characteristics I want to strengthen in myself, skills I want to improve, and ideas I want to be part of has allowed me to "sneak up" on growth.

In this recent reflection on the role growth has played in my life and my relationship to the concept, I had somewhat of an aha moment connected to how and when I label something as a growth experience. Looking back on my journey, I was trying to pinpoint moments when I made the proactive, intentional decision toward growth. To push myself outside of my comfort zone. To risk being bad at something first. In my initial reflection, I almost entirely ignored the events and situations— like divorce, co-parenting, family health crises—that I did not choose for myself but had to navigate and manage.

When I have less agency in the decision to invite a growth opportunity into my life, I am less likely to recognize the growth, resilience, intention, tenacity, courage, strength, acceptance, love, etc., that it took to navigate. I can quickly go, as many privileged people do, to dismissing experiences as challenging because there are many examples of those whose lives are much more dire. In my circumstances, admitting stress or struggle can sometimes seem petty. It is often difficult to find the right balance between pushing myself to rise to the challenge and extending grace to myself when the bandwidth for personal growth is narrow.

Part of that grace has also been developing a healthier definition of growth. Growth is not always linear. This cognitive shift was critical to my mental health. Like many people, I initially tended to only label or reward things that looked like forward progress. Anything that felt stagnant, or a step backward, would bring discomfort, disappointment, and anxiety. It was labeled at best inefficient and at worst catastrophic to my path in life. Finding patience and recognizing the importance of these times has allowed me to experience important journeys I never could have planned. I've learned that when we feel we are regressing or becoming stagnant, we are often being prepared for future growth. More than we tend to acknowledge, our journey includes "slingshot" periods, when we are pulled in the opposite direction, resulting in focused velocity in our path forward.

Not only can "regression" and "stagnation" play a critical, positive role in one's life, but so can disruption and destruction. We've all experienced that moment in organizing a room when it becomes much more chaotic and messier than when we started, but eventually we get to our desired outcome. Our paths to being our better selves deserve the same grace and patience. Our world of photo filters and life events staged for social media, not to mention our society's intolerance for missteps and its propensity for public shaming, sends the message that a messy path shouldn't be tolerated. Acknowledging the value and beauty of the mess can add peace to our inner voices, and more authenticity in our world.

Spending my days in the world of innovation and entrepreneurship—where disruption, messiness, and change are ever present—has enriched my personal evolution. It has also made me an advocate for journey transparency. Many startup founders begin their work naïve about the challenges. Fueled by pop culture's focus on the "highs," they are unprepared for the proverbial roller coaster that is a startup founder's life. Even as ecosystem builders we are quick to use the adage "we learn more from our failures than we do from our successes," yet struggle to be publicly transparent as to how messy the journey is in the business of disruption. Finding moments to allow "behind the curtain" access to the complicated journeys in your world can often have more positive impact than the opposite. This knowledge of the power of transparency is a key reason I chose to take part in this anthology series. The vulnerability required in this process opens a door for powerful connection and collaborative growth that 100 percent polished, filtered slivers of one's life never will.

Going through this process of analyzing the thoughts and behaviors that drive my relationship with growth has been a rewarding and enlightening one. And it is in the spirit of connection through transparency and authenticity that I share my journey. I look forward to continuing to strengthen my ability to engage and celebrate diverse growth avenues. I encourage you to stay open to how growth opportunities show up for you. Give yourself permission to explore them with varied amounts of preparation and expectation. Growth comes in many forms, through many journeys, and at a variety of speeds. May you find moments to energetically dive in, as well as declare, "I don't have the bandwidth for personal growth today," with a peace rooted in the truth that those moments are just as valuable.

Melissa Grizzle has played an integral role in building the innovation eco-system in the St. Louis region over the past twenty-five years, beginning in the corporate setting with Monsanto's Mergers & Acquisitions and New Product Launch teams, then as an original employee of BioGenerator, the life science seed fund now a part of BioSTL. Joining the management team of the cleantech startup, Akermin, Melissa spent almost a decade riding the startup journey roller coaster, accumulating knowledge, networks, and wisdom. In 2014 Melissa joined the entrepreneurial support organization, ITEN (Innovation, Technology & Entrepreneur Network) as Director of Entrepreneur Development where she has become a champion for entrepreneurs exploring and launching new innovative companies.

In 2020, ITEN became a division of Lindenwood University, merging Melissa's two passions of the innovation community and higher education. Raised in college towns by parents in academia, Melissa holds degrees in Educational Psychology and Higher Education Administration from the University of Missouri, as well as a degree in American Sign Language Interpreting from St. Louis Community College–Florissant Valley.

www.linkedin.com/in/melissagrizzle/
www.twitter.com/melissagrizzle

Linda Goldstein

"You've Come a Long Way, Baby!"

(Virginia Slims Cigarettes Advertising Slogan)

The Backstory

Backstories are always interesting, aren't they? Every journey has its ups and downs, and we're stronger and smarter as a result of overcoming obstacles. Here's the story behind one of my biggest challenges and the leadership lessons I learned from it.

As a child growing up in Chicago, I had dreams and plans for my future just like every other little girl. But I never imagined that I would be elected the first woman mayor of Clayton, Missouri, and that for most of my career I would run a flooring company in the predominantly male commercial construction industry.

I've become stronger as a leader and feel good about my successes in both politics and business, but my biggest challenge and most proud moment was when Clayton passed its Clean-Air Ordinance.

Ideas are fueled by passion. Passion is what drives us to work tirelessly so that a cause greater than ourselves can become a reality.

My passion and persistence as mayor resulted in Clayton passing smoking legislation that set off a domino effect resulting in St. Louis City and County following our lead and restricting smoking in public spaces.

Here's my story.

Shortly after I was elected mayor, I learned that one of the reasons many of our young people were not coming back to the St. Louis area after college was because smoking was allowed in restaurants and other public areas. This, along with the hazards of secondhand smoke and health risks of smoking, inspired me to take on the challenge of clean-air legislation.

It wasn't that I wanted to tell people they couldn't smoke, but that they couldn't smoke in places where their passive smoke would harm others. People who weren't smoking shouldn't have to breathe smoke-filled air and have their health compromised by another person's actions. This perspective is similar to alcohol-impaired driving legislation. No one says you can't drink; you just can't drink and drive.

I started at the Missouri state level but essentially was laughed out of Jefferson City. Then I went to the county but couldn't get any traction there either. My next attempt was to meet with four other mayors from surrounding municipalities and ask them to band together to make the inner-ring suburbs smoke-free. They agreed, but one by one they all dropped out because their elected boards would not agree to take on the challenge.

Finally, I went back to my Board of Aldermen and asked if they were willing to go smoke-free even if Clayton was an island. The right to breathe clean air seems like a no-brainer now, doesn't it? But at the time it was hugely controversial, and my board had the political courage to say, "Yes! It's the right thing to do for public health. We're in!" I was, and am, so proud of those elected officials!

We carefully planned a process that took almost eight months. We wanted to make sure we did it right. We wanted to hear from our residents, businesses, restaurants, and health professionals and organizations.

Our first move was to conduct a survey of our residents, property owners, businesses, hotels, and restaurants. The data showed that 76 percent of our residents and a majority of our businesses and hotels wanted Clayton to go smoke-free. Our eighty-plus restaurants were almost evenly split "for" and "against" clean-air legislation. As with every other controversial issue, the opposition was very vocal; there was tremendous pressure on us by some of the restaurant owners not to pass a smoking ban.

Armed with data and a carefully crafted plan, we began a series of outreach meetings and public hearings.

Things got off to a good start, but then...

There was the night I drove up to City Hall for one of our public hearings and, as usual, the media trucks and satellite dishes were all over. This time, though, there were people picketing in front the building. Cars drove by honking. My first thought was, "It's going to be a very long night," but as I got closer I saw that the picketers were all wearing Clayton High School tee shirts and the signs they carried said "HONK IF YOU WANT CLEAN AIR." You can't imagine how proud I was of those students! I wanted young people to get involved in politics, and here they were expressing themselves and joining the process. As we moved forward, we had more little wins like Clayton high schoolers picketing.

Behind the scenes, I was getting some *very interesting* emails. A number of restaurant owners were unwilling to speak out publicly, but they urged us for a variety of reasons to adopt a Clean Air Ordinance. One individual's email began, "My wife and I eat dinner in Clayton restaurants all the time. I'm a smoker and after every meal light up a cigarette. If you ban smoking," (I thought... *Uh-oh, here we go!*) "I'll have to go outside to smoke and I won't do that. And that's a good thing since I really should cut down. So I'll still come to your restaurants. I just wanted to let you know that I support what you're doing about banning smoking."

Despite the sensational media coverage throughout our community engagement, we had productive meetings with the restaurants and other constituents. Based on the input, we modified the draft ordinance so that it addressed their concerns, and we also cleared up misconceptions about the proposed legislation. Everyone felt respected and was happy that we were truly listening to them.

Our conversations with the restaurants helped us understand their serious concerns. We finally had modified the draft ordinance to their satisfaction and pledged money for a PR campaign to roll out Clayton's new smoke-free dining in our many wonderful restaurants.

The restaurant group approved the modified ordinance, but their spokesperson continued to publicly rail against it. I finally sat down with him one-on-one to ask why he was sending the message that the sky would fall if people couldn't smoke in his restaurant. He said, "There's no way I could ever afford this kind of publicity. I'm interviewed on the news every night and quoted in the newspaper every day!" "Yes," I agreed, "but you might want to change your message."

HIM: "Why?"

ME: "Because you're telling the world the only reason people go to your restaurant is to smoke…apparently, they don't come for your food."

HIM: "Hmm…you've got a good point."

The next day his message was: "I've been working closely with the City of Clayton, and I'm pleased with their changes to the ordinance. People come to my restaurant because of our delicious food and great service, not to smoke. Implementing this revised clean-air ordinance will not hurt my business. In fact, I'm expecting my business to increase."

Our Clean-Air Ordinance passed unanimously after a very civil and inclusive public process.

Meanwhile, I had been working with Lyda Krewson, who, at that time, was a St. Louis City Alderman and later became the first woman mayor of St. Louis. Lyda was successful in getting legislation passed designating that if the county went smoke-free, so would the city. I also worked with Barbara Frasier, a St. Louis County Councilwoman, whose efforts resulted in the smoke-free issue being put on the ballot. A vote of the county residents was overwhelmingly in support of clean-air legislation.

That's the story of how the City of Clayton blazed the trail for clean air and public health. And how three strong women—Lyda Krewson, Barbara Frasier, and I—made the St. Louis region smoke-free.

We can make things happen even if we must go it alone, but when we band together we can really make a difference! "Never believe that a few caring people can't change the world. For, indeed, that's all who ever have." – Margaret Mead

Lessons Learned

After every big project in my business or political service, I would always convene my team for a debrief. We would analyze whether we achieved our goal, look at what happened during the process, and summarize our lessons learned.

I made my own list of Leadership Lessons Learned, and here are some of my takeaways from my quest to improve public health in the St. Louis region.

Research, Research, Research! We had lots of data from multiple sources about the health risks of smoking and passive smoke, the overwhelming support for a smoking ban in our community, and the economic impact of smoke-free legislation in other cities.

You can't make everyone happy; be respectful but don't be afraid to disagree. We gathered input from all parties involved to make sure that the consideration of a smoking ban was an inclusive process. The ordinance that we passed was a result of our research and public input.

"One plus one equals more than two." Identify and work with allies, like-minded people who also believe in your cause. It's the power of one versus the power of the group; collaboration is key to success.

Have a sense of humor; stay grounded; maintain your focus. This was one of the most challenging projects my board and I had ever undertaken. When the controversy and nay-saying became too much for any of us, we helped each other through the crisis with a little humor and the reminder of the importance of our work.

Be confident; embrace your skills; step outside your comfort zone. In other words, "Follow your passion!"

We certainly have "come a long way, baby!"

Linda Goldstein is Founder/CEO of Linda Goldstein Consulting LLC; former Mayor of the City of Clayton, Missouri; and coach and trusted advisor to CEOs, business leaders, owners, and other key executives.

With more than twenty years of multi-disciplinary senior-level leadership roles, Linda draws on her experience in the private, public, and nonprofit sectors to help her clients become better leaders and grow their organizations.

For six consecutive years, the *St. Louis Business Journal* recognized Linda as one of the Most Influential St. Louisans, and she was also named as one of the 25 Most Influential Women in Business. Linda has a master's degree in Counseling Psychology from St. Louis University and a Bachelor of Science degree in Public Relations from the University of Illinois.

www.LindaGoldsteinConsulting.com
www.linkedin.com/in/lindalgoldstein/
www.twitter.com/LindaGoldstein

Jennifer Church

True Colors

Once upon a time there was a blonde-haired, blue-eyed little girl who set her sights on the fairy tale. I just knew life would be like all those bedtime stories and no matter what there would be a happy ending. As a preteen and throughout my fifty years, so far, I have learned everything doesn't always work out, there are no magic wands, and fairy dust doesn't make you fly.

Each of us have had our own trials, tribulations, and people who negatively affected our lives. Unfortunately, if I listed the adversities I have faced in my life, I could fill this entire chapter. Those people or experiences used to consume me; they shaped who I was. Thankfully, because I have experienced the blessing of *growth*, they will be given zero attention, no glory, and receive no more energy from me ever again. I have come to see each of the people in my life as one of my crayons.

If life is a canvas and we are the artist, coloring the most beautiful picture we can, then each of the people we encounter can be seen as crayons. Stay with me on this. If you had a box of crayons to color an award-winning picture, or to provide a picture of a well-lived life, you certainly would want the biggest box of crayons they make, to have the most variety, the most depth, and the best way to highlight the important parts. You would try to color the most beautiful picture, right?

I have learned to look at life as a blank canvas, *tabula rasa*. I relate to this image because I have a fancy for art and can hold my own artistically. In the world of art or in everyday life, it's possible to create something, anything you want, out of the tools you have. Throughout life, your journey is to create the most beautiful picture you can and share your picture with others.

When I was a teenager, I had a small box of crayons. I believed that the fewer people you let in, the less people could hurt you, and the fewer things could go wrong or be taken away. After years and years of using the same small box of crayons, my picture was listless and bland. It lacked energy and was filled with primary colors, not much contrast, and completely ordinary. This picture would never be museum quality nor be imitated by other artists. I knew I had to start looking at things differently. I had to surround myself with people who had a more vivid picture so that I could learn from them, replicate them, and continue to maintain forward progress. So that is what I did.

I tried to learn something from every person I encountered: their body language, their charisma, their knowledge of things, the way they made people feel. Whatever they put out there, I tried to understand. I looked at each of them as one of my crayons, one of the varieties I could use to color my picture. With my love of art, I also knew that there are hundreds of shades of each color. I looked for them all within the people I chose to surround myself with, so I could color my masterpiece, better known as my life.

The primary crayons are the people closest to you, those whom you can't imagine life without. You must have primary colors to make ever other color that exists. They are essential. Your primary color people are most likely your parents, siblings, significant other, and your children.

They are the foundation of everything you cherish. They make up every part of your picture in some way or another.

Secondary colors are made from the primary colors. They are a mix of colors. These people are very close to you: a cousin, a mentor, your friends, close acquaintances. These are people you share a bond with, interact with often, aspire to be like, or share similar interests with. Secondary colors incorporate the primary colors and spin off into another beautiful shade to color your picture. Throughout your life, you will inevitably have a core group of these crayons in your box. If you are fortunate, as I am, these crayons will surround you. They will be the part of your everyday life and be a major part of your picture. They will teach you love, patience, compassion. They will encourage you and offer guidance.

From there, tertiary colors—which means the in-between colors, all the other colors—are made. The tertiary people colors would be coworkers, neighbors, and team members, coaches, the lady in line at the grocery store next to you, your mailman, someone who belongs to the same organization as you, etc. These are the people who may need your help with a task such as unloading their grocery cart, or maybe just a simple smile or "thank you" as you walk past them. They may be there to teach you a new skill, show you a better way, or lead you to a new path. They may or may not be someone you share your life with, but they are still a part of your story. They are still a crayon in your box. They aren't the colors you use very often, but they keep the picture balanced. They are the background colors.

Now, you don't have to be a fan of all the people you meet. But those people are put on your path for a reason. There are still lessons to learn from them. Perhaps what you take from them is nothing more than what you don't want to do or choose not to mimic in your picture. These people are still a very valuable crayon. They are the contrast. They create the shadows in your picture and give it depth. With these colors, you realize that everything in life is not yellow sunshine and bright blue skies. There are times that things are dark and dim. This is when you color the shadows in your picture, take the lesson from that, and try move on to the next brighter part of your picture. Without contrast, your picture wouldn't have key elements of dimension.

Someday, if you are lucky, you'll find the crayon that is the highlight. This crayon is usually a few shades brighter than the main color source. It, too, is a contrast, but it brightens the picture and adds the correct emphasis on the part that matters. It takes an artist years and years to know exactly how to use the highlight in the appropriate way and, most importantly, in the appropriate place. The highlight makes your picture a perfectly well-rounded masterpiece. This crayon, if you have done things correctly, represents you, your children, or is the brightness you receive from your spouse or partner. This crayon is the one that shines the light on the perfect part of every piece of your story.

All your crayons are invaluable because your picture is composed of every single crayon you have kept in your box. Every time you meet someone, find their color, figure out what it means to you, and place it carefully in your box so that someday when the time is right you can reflect on that color and use it in your picture to bring color to your story and allow someone else to discover the shade of color within you. It may be just what they have been looking for.

I am truly blessed to have the most amazing daughter, Morgan. She is one of my highlights. My wonderful family has been there through the highlights and the shadows. They are my primary colors. My foundation. I have such a fabulous group of friends, and there are so many colors within that group. I am so grateful for the privilege to be at a Fortune 500 company for twenty years, at this point. I have picked up so many crayons here and in our industry. This is where the contrast crayons have played the biggest part. I have had the honor of serving on a board of directors where I learned that the boldest crayon and the palest crayon both hold value. Bold colors don't always need to be the forefront of your picture, and the pale crayon that sits quietly off to the side is the one that adds the best hue or shading to the picture.

So here is what this grown-up, fairy tale–dreaming little girl has learned: Scoop up every crayon you can, get the biggest box to hold them, and color the most beautiful picture. Then, decide what color crayon you want to be and be that color for someone else's crayon box. Remember that without growth, there is no progress. Color the best picture you can imagine; your possibilities are endless.

Jennifer currently resides in St. Louis, Missouri, where she was born and raised. Morgan, her daughter, is her greatest love. She is in the role of Strategic Account Manager with United Rentals, a Fortune 500 company that she has called home for twenty years. She is a past president of the American Subcontractors Association Midwest Council. Her hobbies include family, golf, boating, and art.

www.linkedin.com/in/jennifer-church-61345911a/
www.facebook.com/profile.php?id=100082698759265
www.instagram.com/JenniferRChurch/

Shequana Hughes

Impaired to Blooming

Impaired

Depression and anxiety are a bitch…or are they?

"Mom, it's happening again," I whispered into the phone. My mom answered my call for what seemed like the tenth time that month and heard my voice, laced with desperation and tears. "I can't take this anymore," I muttered.

"Do you need me?" she asked.

"Yes," was the only response I could muster before she hung up and arrived twenty-five minutes later. The door opened and I fell into her arms before she could see the sorrow in my eyes.

"What do you think is the issue?" she asked.

"I really don't know, but I think I need to go to the emergency room," I replied. "I can't sleep, and I feel like I'm dying. I can't breathe."

"You don't want just to lay down?" she asked. "There may be nothing they can do." *Like all the other times before, I'm sure she was thinking.*

"I know. I'd just like to be sure." As we headed out the door, my best friend arrived with a look of helplessness on her face. I kissed my children as if it would be the last time (like every time before). Again, I was headed to a place I hated but found the most comfort and felt the safest in—the emergency room. I knew I'd lost it.

My mom pulled into the emergency room entrance and parked, and I dragged myself out of the car and through the revolving doors. Suddenly, I stopped and turned around, headed back to the car. "I can't keep doing this," I said, but it was too late. I was there, and we both knew I wouldn't get any rest until I'd been seen. So, reluctantly, I made my way to the receptionist desk to disclose my "issues."

After I was all checked in and ready to see the doctor, just like all the other times, my racing heart slowed, my mind calmed, and the sleep that had escaped me for the past three nights returned. But before I could close my eyes, a white-haired man with a bright smile knocked on the door and stepped into the tiny patient room. He instantly put me more at ease. "Mrs. Hughes, how can I help you tonight?" he asked.

"I don't know, I just haven't been feeling well and would like to get checked out." *Fix me, please,* I was actually thinking.

He asked a question that I'd heard before, but not quite the way I heard it this time. "Have there been any significant changes in your life lately that could be causing you stress?" *Heartache was more like it.*

"Yes," I barely got out. "My husband and I separated six months ago, and I have been taking care of my five children alone since then. Nothing major." I laughed, trying to lighten the mood.

"OK, try to relax," he said. "I suggest we do a complete workup, and that you stay overnight." That was a first. He glanced over at my mom and said with a smile, "Just to put her mind at ease."

"Is there anything you can give her to relax her?" she asked.

"Sure, I'll send the nurse in," he replied. After the nurse administered the medication, my mom climbed into bed with me and rocked me to sleep as if I were her five-year-old baby girl again. I think that may have been more soothing than the medication I had just received. It wasn't long before I was fast asleep.

The next morning, as promised, I received a full workup: stress test... check, EKG...check, bloodwork...check. All the while, I could think of any other place I'd rather be than in the hospital. By that afternoon, I was given a clean bill of health and at least thirty-five years left to live. All good to hear, but I knew if I continued on this path, I wouldn't make it that long. Something had to give. As I walked out the same doors I had entered not even twenty-four hours earlier, I vowed this would not be my life. I put the ER behind me.

Blooming

At home that night, I came to terms with the love I had lost and created a much-needed plan for what I wanted my life to look like going forward. I knew that to overcome what I had been going through, a transformation had to happen. For the next year, I visualized, prayed, meditated, and talked to those closest to me about my plans to *move forward* and where I could use their support. I needed to improve my health (mentally and physically). I started by taking a short walk each day, changed some things in my diet, and I made an appointment with a therapist. I discovered that I had been suffering from anxiety and depression and was prescribed medication to help me cope with the mental hell/illness I had been experiencing.

There was also that thriving business I needed to get a handle on. I realized I could no longer do things alone and hired contractors to assist in creating better organizational structure and support. I contacted a mentor to help me navigate my role as CEO.

If you haven't noticed, there's a common theme throughout my blooming period. I knew that I could not bloom alone. From my family and friends to the team of professionals I'd hired, to my therapist and mentor, my tribe was the only way I would be able to see this through. I would love to say that the feeling of hopelessness and despair never visited me again after that night in the emergency room, but on the days that I just couldn't get out of bed, I now had a future to look forward to. I remembered what I wanted, where I was headed, and how I was going to get there.

Today, five years later, I woke up to a change of scenery, in a nice sunny place I'd always dreamed of living (a part of my plan was to move out of state), with the people I love most surrounding me (including my husband, but that's a story for another anthology). My days are designed by me, and my systems and operations firm is a well-organized machine. My panic attacks are few and far between, and hospital visits are null. Each day is a new opportunity for me to bloom. Here's what I learned from my experience:

6. **I was not alone.** I learned while discussing my issues with my family and friends that I was not the only woman who had ever dealt with anxiety and depression. But that's how you feel when you're going through those things. My grandmother shared stories that were very similar to mine. We would sit and talk for hours about her ER visits and fear of dying from what she believed was a heart attack but was, in fact, heartache. These conversations and storytelling helped to alleviate my self-doubt and "less than" feelings. So, share your story; if there is no one close to you that you feel comfortable sharing with, find a trusted resource. They have a professional way of helping you cope with feelings of loneliness and shame. Keeping your feelings hidden is one of the things that will keep you stuck for a lot longer than you have to be. Know that there are people who want you to get better.

7. **Depression is and looks like many different things**. One of these, surprisingly, could be an opportunity to bloom. If you are experiencing an opportunity to bloom, it may be time to do something you've never done, or finish something you started. Remember, the small steps you take each day make the greatest

impact. I started walking just fifteen minutes per day and am now up to four to five miles each day. Talk to a professional. If you've never taken the time to get to know yourself, this may be the time. If you've never rested, rest. If you've never taken a trip alone and you desire to, take that vacation. Move to a different state, remove people from your life who no longer fit. These are all things designed to help you bloom/grow through any storm.

If you are feeling alone, know that you are not. If you are feeling like you are the first woman to experience anxiety and depression, there are many of us. Just like the many women who have gone through or are still going through these issues, you can and will overcome them. Here's to blooming.

Being a wife, a CEO, and a mom of five can make for life and business chaos. So for six years, Shequana Hughes, the CEO and System Strategist at Business Balance Systems, has made it her mission to help mothers who work as coaches, consultants, and service providers create business balance. Helping hundreds of women implement systems, strategies, and software into their life and business in the simplest way possible (Simple Systems) has not only afforded them a business free from chaos but one that allows growth and stability. Shequana recently launched the Business Balance System software, an all-in-one marketing and CRM (Customer Relationship Management) software, a business born through chaos transformed into growth.

www.businessbalancesystem.com
314-339-7449
www.linkedin.com/in/shequana-hughes/
www.facebook.com/shequana.hughes
www.facebook.com/businessbalancesystems
www.instagram.com/businessbalancesystems/

Linda Loewenstein

Cheers!

A Cheerleader: an enthusiastic and vocal supporter of someone or something. Plain and simple, that's me! As a freshman at Affton High School, I made the cheerleading team, and that cheerleader mindset helped shape my life more than I would have ever imagined. To some that may sound a little obnoxious, but it's really about believing you have a winning team, building team spirit, delivering the occasional pep talk, and the post-game celebrations.

My parents were, without a doubt, my biggest cheerleaders. This would make for a more riveting chapter if I had a challenging childhood filled with struggles to succeed, but that's not my story. As an only child, my growing-up years were wonderfully uneventful, focused on having fun and pleasing my parents. Their approval came easily...except that one time:

As an undergrad at University of Missouri–Columbia, known as "Mizzou", I started out studying accounting because my dad was an accountant and he suggested, "Business school is the best place for women in the '70s." After one year, and without telling Mom and Dad, I switched majors to interior design. For the first time in my life, my parents were horrified, disappointed, and confused by my decision. This was long before HGTV, and my parents questioned, "Is this even a career?"

My dad's approval was everything to me. He took his job seriously but never sought accolades. It wasn't until after his death that I learned he was a WWII Bronze Star Recipient for his heroism. He never spoke of it. "Always give it your best (and focus on profit)" was his mantra. After all, he was an accountant!

Fast forward to 1984, and I interviewed for an interior design position at the newly formed Lawrence Group, an architectural firm made up of three best friends from the University of Kansas–Lawrence. Steve Smith, David Ohlemeyer, and Paul Doerner spent four years carpooling back and forth to KU, dreaming of the "Super Firm," hence the name. My initial job responsibilities included typing letters and invoices, answering the phone, greeting guests, and, yes, interior design (department of one). I knew this was a winning team, and it was the best decision I ever made. Shortly after, Laura Conrad joined the firm as CFO, a key role with a team of designers. Years later, our interiors group became the largest in St. Louis, starting with the mentality that *design* was always about the client and helping them realize their dreams. It wasn't always perfect, but there was a mutual trust, admiration, and respect for everyone's strengths that was at the core of the relationship and a key to the firm's early success.

How did we go from a small group of friends in a townhouse in historic Lafayette Square to a nationally recognized multi-office firm of designers and architects? It began with building the best team possible and embracing growth.

While this book is about a growth mindset, I *do not* embrace growth for growth's sake. I fundamentally do not like change. Change has always been extremely uncomfortable for me, and often growth and change go hand in hand. While I disliked change, I tried to focus on the positives on the other side of change, and I realized that I loved the challenge of building the team and growing the organization. Eventually, I no longer viewed change as the enemy but rather the opportunity for growth, and I could get on board with that concept! One of our core values was believing in individual growth and creativity. I focused on hiring people smarter than me, encouraging diversity of thought, giving designers the tools they needed to succeed, and then being their biggest cheerleader!

One of my favorite business sayings is, "Culture will eat strategy for lunch!" Culture is hard to pinpoint from the outside, but once inside, people feel it. We knew ours was unique and felt obligated to cultivate it. Culture is every single person's responsibility in the organization. As we built the team, we laid the foundation of culture by hiring the best possible employees. Our corporate culture was our secret weapon. My goal was to achieve maximum "team spirit," and the tangible results were extremely low employee turnover and extremely high client retention. Our culture created an atmosphere where not just employees, clients, and sales reps but everyone in our business circle was motivated and energized to be part of a winning team. Having fun was one of our core values and a key to our successful culture. In addition to creating a functional design solution and being profitable, we measured fun in our annual reviews. "You can't improve what you don't measure," wrote Peter Drucker.

Building a positive team culture was one challenge, but being a positive cheerleader when the team is down is the real challenge. My mom was the best example of this in my life. She's the most positive person I've ever known. She could have written the best-selling book *The Power of Positive Thinking* by Norman Vincent Peale. She woke up every day and thought, "Something wonderful is going to happen to me today," spent her day looking for it, and went to bed thanking God for it. I relied on that positive attitude even when things seemed hopeless.

The recession of 2008 was devastating to our firm and our entire industry. The architecture industry was desecrated. We had multi-millions in backlog projects and a large, talented team, but it was all put on indefinite hold. We were forced to make painful layoffs and cut hours and pay. Senior leadership went without pay, but that wasn't enough. Like every other design firm, we laid off great people who had nowhere else to go in our field. It was heartbreaking. Everything we worked so hard to build was slipping away.

How could we ever possibly rebuild trust in the organization, rebuild the culture to some semblance of what it had been? The remaining staff was frustrated, and it seemed to many that our decisions were insensitive and random. We took none of the decisions lightly. There simply were no good options. Everything we spent years building seemed to go up in smoke, and there seemed to be no way to put out the fire.

While the design business is always one of the first to slow in a recession, they are also the first to bounce back. Corporations began to see the light at the end of the tunnel and pent-up demand helped douse the flames of the recession fires. We began rebuilding. We spent a lot of time listening to issues, attempting to address them, and making real changes. Although they were angry, many dedicated employees believed in the organization, and, above all else, they wanted to see it succeed again. Thanks to their help, we literally rebuilt the culture brick by brick and brought the fun back.

Keeping a positive attitude during this period was nearly impossible, but I had no choice. I had to look for something wonderful to happen every day and do my best to keep up the positive spirit, just like my mom taught me. Our team looked to the leadership for hope, and we couldn't express the real fear we were facing. With everyone's help, we survived and continued to thrive.

Finally, I must tell you about the post-game celebrations. As we designed the firm, one of our core values was having fun and celebrating everything! In addition to all the parties and big win celebrations, having fun really meant showing appreciation for a job well done. An attitude of gratitude is free to give away and more important than any business card title. It's so important to share appreciation for the person being praised and to communicate that appreciation to others.

My mom was my biggest fan. She had a quiet confidence, and she truly felt like she could do anything. My mom was not confident in an arrogant sort of way, but she was always willing to give things a try and she "knew" it would work out. More importantly, my mom had confidence in others around her and believed in me in the same way. To know that I always had someone who believed in me and had my back was the greatest gift in the world. To have her in my corner, believing I was more than capable and could 100 percent accomplish anything I attempted, was a gift that cannot be measured.

I would like to say I was that person to everyone on our team, but I am quite certain I was not. My intention certainly was to be the cheerleader in the background pulling for each person, rooting for everyone, accepting their failures, and shouting about their successes.

My favorite sports quote is from the Great Gretzky, "You miss 100 percent of the shots you don't take." Did we always put the puck in the back of the net? No, but we were always cheering for each other, and I am beyond blessed to have had supportive parents and to have worked with the best, most talented people in the world.

Linda Loewenstein is a proud Mizzou grad and her role at Lawrence Group included leading the nationally recognized interiors group, owner of Niche Home Furnishings and principal-in-charge of marketing.

In addition to her team's numerous national design awards, Loewenstein has been recognized by the *St. Louis Business Journal* as one of 2003's Most Influential Women, and she's additionally been the recipient of the CREW Career Advancement Award and the Mizzou Citation of Merit Award.

After thirty-one years, Loewenstein retired, but she remains actively involved in her community. Loewenstein is currently on the board of Habitat for Humanity Saint Louis and served as President in 2017 and 2018. She served on the SSM St. Mary's Foundation Board and Mizzou's Architectural Studies Advisory Board for over ten years. She also leads her church's participation in an afterschool program for kids in Ferguson.

In her free time, Linda enjoys keeping active with swimming, cycling, golfing, kayaking, and swing dancing. Linda and John enjoy spending time with their two children, Aly and Joe, and their two grandchildren, Kenzie and Hudson.

www.linkedin.com/in/lindaloewenstein
www.facebook.com/linda.thomsenloewenstein
www.instagram.com/lindaloew3
www.tiktok.com/@swag_..nana

Alana Muller

Discover Your Purpose

"Your calling isn't something that somebody can tell you about. It's what you feel. It is the thing that gives you juice. The thing that you are supposed to do. Nobody can tell you what that is. You know it inside yourself."
– Oprah Winfrey

My life's purpose is to connect, inspire, and empower community. Every business I know of has a mission statement—an inspirational description of what the organization does. The good companies uphold their mission every day by ensuring the work they do honors their mission. Wouldn't it be powerful if individual humans had a personal mission statement—that is, a clear statement of purpose to provide direction and daily guidance? I didn't always understand this concept, but now I wholeheartedly believe it is the thing that can give us a way forward. There is something to be said for figuring out who you are, what you stand for, and pursuing it relentlessly.

I grew up in the Kansas City metropolitan area, where I now make my home. I did stints in Western Massachusetts, New York City, and Chicago before returning to my roots to take a job with a Fortune 40 communications company. After ten years of rising to the executive ranks, I left in search of my entrepreneurial dreams. I took on some consulting assignments and ultimately landed as CEO of a division of a private foundation.

I loved it all and had the privilege of working with inspirational leaders and engaging in meaningful work. I was achieving success and making a difference, yet I lacked intentionality or focused direction.

During my last gig as CEO of Kauffman FastTrac, I was invited by one of my clients to attend an entrepreneurial development retreat in Vail, Colorado. I didn't want to go. I resented this client asking me to give up a precious weekend with my family to attend a silly "kumbaya" session where we would "hug it out." I did everything I could to get out of attending; I even cancelled once. They rescheduled to accommodate my availability. I missed the deadline for my prework. They allowed me to turn it in late. You name it, I was trying to undermine the event.

On the appointed Friday, I reluctantly made my way to a gorgeous little ranch in the Vail Valley. Despite my earlier resistance, I quickly got comfortable with the group. During the weekend, the seven of us did "values identification exercises." Nobody escaped without sharing a few deeply personal stories, shedding some tears, engaging in loads of laughter, and, indeed, growing emotionally and spiritually.

Around noon on Sunday, our facilitator, Karah, announced, "Congratulations, team, we're at the final exercise of the weekend. I'm going to give you thirty minutes, and in five words or fewer, state your life's purpose." Now, here's the thing: Had she told us at the beginning we'd be articulating our life's purpose, I probably would have left rather than engage in such a ridiculous task. However, after experiencing the growth of the prior forty-eight hours, it took me about thirty seconds to write mine. Karah looked at me and said, "OK, hotshot, I can see that you've finished before we've even begun. What did you write?"

I took a deep breath, looked her in the eye, and announced, "My life's purpose is to connect, inspire, and empower community." She looked back at me and said, "Yes, it is. You can get your stuff and go." Stunned, I blinked twice, then burst into tears.

Connect, inspire, and empower community. I had discovered my life's purpose. Suddenly, all the parts of my life gelled together. Everything came into focus. Every prior experience had prepared me for seeing my life's purpose. And by establishing, nurturing, and facilitating meaningful, authentic relationships through networking—the primary way that I was connecting, inspiring, and empowering community—I was afforded professional, community-oriented, and social opportunities beyond my wildest imagination.

I became highly motivated to begin living my truth as quickly as possible; in fact, not doing so felt like a waste of time, energy, and resources. It was time to make some changes and I needed to:

- Get my family on board
- Get real about my priorities and expectations
- Reassess my career
- Think big
- Devise a plan
- Garner support
- Jump in
- Start a movement

All these tasks were accomplished within about nine months, which allowed me to quit my job, reshuffle my schedule, and get busy connecting, inspiring, and empowering community with every action I took. Like a corporate mission statement, I aspire to test every activity I engage in against my personal life's purpose. If the activity is not helping me to connect, inspire, and empower community, I should not be doing it. Sometimes I fail—this is a journey and a process. By having a purpose, when I do make mistakes, I am able to quickly course correct.

Ready to get started on a personal mission statement? Consider these five steps to zero-in on your own life's purpose:

Step 1: Consider your past.

Step 2: Determine your core values.

Step 3: Think about where you currently are vs. where you'd like to go—and be honest! You need to close the gap.

Step 4: Articulate your life's purpose.

Step 5: Pursue your purpose with vigor, with confidence, and with maniacal focus!

Let's take each in turn. First, **consider your past**. Think of the timeline of your life. Identify the high points, the low points, and anything in between that has had a significant impact on the person you are today. Think not only of your accomplishments but of the times you stumbled and the way in which you got up and moved forward on your path.

Next, **determine your core values**. What's important to you? Is it family, service, wealth, relationships, or influence? Be real with yourself. If you say, for example, that family is your most important core value but never spend time with your family, can you really claim it as your #1 core value?

The third part of the process is to **think about where you are vis-à-vis where you'd like to go**. To get there, consider your strengths, your gifts, and your talents. Finish thought starters like "I'm really good at…," "I'm passionate about…," and "I get energized by…" Then, close the gap. Now that you've confirmed where you are and outlined where you'd like to go, design a path to get there. Based on your answers, finish the next sentence with either an "and" statement or a "but" statement. For example, "*I'm passionate about* becoming a social media influencer, *but* I don't know how to take a video on my mobile phone." Time for some lessons. By outlining your strengths, gifts, and talents and thinking through next steps, you will be able to close the gap between where you are now and where you'd like to go.

Now you're ready to **state your life's purpose**. Once you have had honest conversations with yourself about what matters to you, what your values are, and where you want to go, your purpose will naturally reveal itself. Here are a few suggestions for a solid purpose statement:

Why are YOU here? As for me, I'm here to connect, inspire, and empower community.

What is YOUR inspirational reason for being? For me, it's all about connecting people. I believe that building meaningful, authentic relationships makes us happier in business and in life. What is your reason?

Can you capture your purpose with a compelling phrase? When I received my assignment to state my life's purpose, the instructions were to create a statement of five words or fewer. Think of it this way: it ought to fit on a t-shirt! You'll want to know it by heart, and others ought to know it about you.

What is at your CORE? Finally, your purpose statement ought to come from the deepest level of your soul. It is foundational to your very being and is unlikely to change over time. So, while you may alter the tactical approach you take to realizing your purpose, the purpose itself will remain intact.

Now: **Pursue! Pursue! Pursue!**

So, I ask you this: What is *your* life's purpose? Get clear on this as quickly as possible. Reflecting on my fateful weekend in Colorado, the seven of us at that retreat each responded to the assignment with our own five-word (give or take a few words) life's purpose. Within a year, every one of us had begun to pursue our individual purpose and had already achieved success toward our mission.

I wish you success on your life's journey. I encourage you to discover and pursue your life's purpose. It is the way that you will achieve infinite, exponential growth, now and into the future. May you grow from strength to strength.

"We all have a purpose in life, and
when you find yours you will recognize it."
– Catherine Pulsifer

Alana Muller, an entrepreneurial executive leader whose primary focus is to connect, inspire, and empower community, is Founder and CEO of Coffee Lunch Coffee. She is a networking speaker, workshop facilitator, strategist, coach, and author of the book *Coffee Lunch Coffee: A Practical Field Guide for Master Networking* and a companion blog, CoffeeLunchCoffee.com. Her accessible, relevant, immediately actionable approach to professional networking has helped thousands of people formulate a strategic mindset around networking while creating a game plan to get out there and connect. Alana is passionate about working with professionals who are interested in connecting with others, getting involved in their communities, seeking to advance their careers, or looking to build social relationships.

Alana is the host of Enterprise.ing podcast, a weekly columnist for Bizwomen.com, and has been a contributor to Forbes.com, The Huffington Post, CNBC and other publications, and was a featured speaker at TEDx Overland Park. She has an MBA from the University of Chicago and an undergraduate degree in mathematics from Smith College. She is actively engaged in the community and serves on several corporate and volunteer boards.

www.CoffeeLunchCoffee.com
blog.coffeelunchcoffee.com/
www.linkedin.com/in/alanamuller/
www.facebook.com/CoffeeLunchCoffee
www.twitter.com/AlanaMuller

Sheila Burkett

Gaining Courage Through Introspection

My mother swears I came out of the womb driven to get what I want. Over the years, I focused my internal drive on learning. As a student, I quickly got through school material so I could learn through experiences. Growth, to me, is having the courage to do something that challenges you. Through introspection, I've learned to understand my needs as a human being and how to create a fulfilled life. Leaving my corporate job to become an entrepreneur was one of those moments where introspection gave me the courage to make the leap.

This moment was my forty-year-old mid-life crisis, the result of personal growth on my part and the tremendous growth of the company I worked for. After twenty years, I discovered I was restless, unhappy, and saw no long-term career path that fulfilled my passions. This revelation came after an endless series of personality and intelligence tests, part of our company's succession plan process to identify future top leaders. I thought I wanted to be one of those leaders, and that everyone expected this of me. I will never forget when the psychologist reviewed my results. The doctor said, "Are you unhappy?" I answered cautiously, "Why?" She continued, "Your results show you are an entrepreneur. The company today must be crushing your soul, based on how they are operating. Why aren't you in one of their start-up operations?"

I was both stunned and relieved. I realized that who I was as a person didn't align with my "lifer" status. That moment was one of the most pivotal in my life.

These test results gave me new information about how I think, make decisions, and what type of environment I need to be successful. My confidence to explore new options grew. After long discussions with my husband, I decided to quit my job. He had started a small business the previous year, and we had an opportunity to expand it. Knowing I needed change, I confidently resigned from my corporate job to run our race and performance car business. Imagine the surprise of my boss, peers, and team to hear that I was leaving a very good job with significant benefits to run my own business! That leap required me to tap into my principles and values, which I discovered by gaining insight into myself as a person.

Stephen Covey's books guided me to think about my principles and values. My maternal grandparents introduced me to the importance of behavior and basing decisions on foundational beliefs. They were disciplined, principled people who lived their lives in a kind and giving way. As I reflected on my decisions, actions, and my grandparents' impact, I realized there was more to life than financial and business success. My relationships with my husband, kids, family, and friends were very important to me. Making a difference in my community and helping others realize their potential brought me joy.

I didn't learn these values in school. During my corporate career, the company's focus on core values gave me an understanding of how to balance personal values with career goals. My core values help me navigate my life and contribute to my success as an entrepreneur. They gave me the courage to make changes, say no, and speak up.

My first core value is to always be open to learning and to recognize I do not know everything. This doesn't mean going back to school. The key is to gain knowledge and a deeper understanding of topics that may advance your career, open doors to new opportunities, or expand your views on the world. Throughout my career, I found opportunities to learn new skills. When I started my own business, I had to learn about social media, setting up an eCommerce store, running Google Ads, and website development. I learned about engine management systems, how to sell race fuel, and how to navigate local, state, and federal laws. Those skills ultimately led me to cofound Spry Digital. Each day I learned new concepts, developed new skills, and honed those that are critical to successful leadership. As a first-time CEO, I lean into what I know and acknowledge the things I don't. I surround myself with people who are smarter than me and have different backgrounds, experiences, and expertise. When I don't have the budget for a full-time skill or role, I embrace outsourcing to experts such as accountants, human resource professionals, or business consultants.

Being a lifetime learner does not mean everything you learn has to be related to your profession or industry. When I learned to drive a race car, I did it for me. I faced my fears and learned more about cars. Imagine the excitement of being in a group of thirty race cars as the green flag is thrown! When I drove in my first race, it took everything I had to stay in the pack as I was bumped from behind and as I fought to move up. Over the years, I've continued to take workshops, read, and participate in discussions around social justice, diversity, equity, inclusion, and accessibility. Creating a community and workplace where everyone feels they belong is important to me. Tapping into my continuous learner core value gives me the drive to push through the uncomfortable reality that what I thought I knew is not necessarily the truth. I grapple with unwiring my brain and finding my own unconscious bias.

Albert Einstein once said, "Once you stop learning, you start dying."

The second core value that drives me is giving to others and to the community. While at the University of Missouri–St. Louis, I became a Delta Zeta. As a sorority member, I discovered the personal rewards from giving my time, talent, and money. As a female leader in technology for over thirty years and the leader of a business, I know the importance of being a visible role model to other women. I treasure the mentoring I've received from both men and women throughout my career. They give me the courage to pursue roles I'm not 100 percent ready to take on and provide me guidance as I navigate life. This is why I happily mentor others. I feel joy as I listen to new founders, share their challenges, and give them encouragement to continue their journey. As I talk to individuals pursuing a career in technology, I'm filled with hope. When I can give my time or talents, I support organizations that align with my personal and professional views. I continue to explore myself to give voice to issues that matter to me, though I lack the courage to discuss them publicly. I'm working to own my voice and the influence I have to make a difference in our world.

So, to each of you, I say this: Find a person whom you can encourage, mentor, and guide through their life journey. Connect with your passion and share your talents with them. This will provide perspective and purpose beyond your job.

The last core value is self-awareness and reflection. Knowing our strengths is easy. Identifying and acknowledging our weaknesses is the hard part. Becoming self-aware and understanding how we affect the world helps us grow. After reading Daniel Goleman's book, Emotional Intelligence, self- and social awareness became a goal of mine. I took more personality tests. Now, I look carefully at myself and how I react to people and situations. I've learned I must slow down and give more background to help people trust my decisions. Active listening goes a long way when working in a team and in personal relationships. I continue to work on being present to others, as I am addicted to multitasking!

Reflecting on our emotions and feelings, identifying triggers, and being able to control ourselves in those situations is empowering. Insightfulness leads to realizing how we are communicating with others. Don't get me wrong—people still push my buttons, and some days it isn't easy to control my reactions. We are human, and that happens. But by increasing my emotional intelligence, I have become a compassionate leader, wife, mother, friend, and person.

I believe I can be my authentic self and feel comfortable with who I am, how I live my life, how I lead, and how I follow because of my core values. My willingness to learn, to give to others, and to be self-reflective creates the space to love and accept myself. Through my authentic self, I gain the confidence I need to navigate uncertainty, tackle new challenges, and say no to things that don't bring me joy.

As you consider "What can I do to make my journey a little smoother?", I hope these suggestions will be of value. Embrace being a lifelong learner. Find a way to give of your time, talents, and money. Look within yourself and grow as a person. May these three values help you have a long, successful career and rewarding life.

Sheila Burkett, founder and CEO at Spry Digital, is an advocate for diversity in technology, and a dynamic networker. With Sheila's leadership, Spry Digital made the 2021 Inc 5000 Fastest Growing Company List, after Sheila earned the distinction of Women's Foundation of Greater St. Louis Women in the Workplace Honoree in both 2019 and 2020.

Spry Digital's unique combination of resources work together to strategize, design, and develop web platform and online revenue channels with the best user outcomes in mind. They understand that successful technical solutions require a human touch. Each project launched is a step toward a more inclusive, effective, and usable digital landscape for all.

Sheila and her husband, Steven, have three adult sons and two daughters-in-law. She has her Bachelor of Science in Business Administration from the University of Missouri–St. Louis and a Master in Business Administration from Washington University. Sheila serves on multiple boards, associations, and alumni organizations.

www.linkedin.com/in/sheilaburkett/
www.linkedin.com/company/spry-digital-llc/
www.facebook.com/SpryDigital
www.instagram.com/saburkett/
www.instagram.com/sprydigital/
www.twitter.com/saburkett
www.twitter.com/SpryDigital

Kimberly Vissak

You are Good Enough!

I am a very private person. I am not one to share information about myself, so when I was asked to write a chapter for this book, my initial thought was, "Wow, you want me...why me?"

Then the feelings moved to "Wait...you want me to tell a story about myself for the world to read?" I felt uncomfortable and a little scared, yet those feelings quickly moved to me realizing this was a great opportunity to grow. The reality is, *if you're comfortable, you're probably not growing.*

When I was young, I was diagnosed with dyslexia. I am not sure if the school I attended was unfamiliar with this diagnosis, or if how I was treated was their approach to supporting a student with dyslexia. Whatever the case, their approach did not fit my needs, although I did not realize the impact it had on me and how I would approach situations until only a few years ago.

Even though dyslexia was identified in 1877, it wasn't until the '90s that they disproved any correlation between dyslexia and intelligence. I struggled in school; it was my understanding from my teachers it was because I was dyslexic. I was excused from math classes and told by a teacher that it was OK if I did not do well on spelling tests because of my learning disability. I believe the teachers were trying to help, but I remember feeling stupid, that I was not good enough, nor would I ever amount to anything.

"You are not good enough." Five little words that, when used separately, are nonthreatening, but when combined can really mess with one's mental state. I'm guessing everyone reading this can relate, whether these are words someone told you or an internal feeling. I can still remember the day, where I was, and exactly what chair I was sitting in when a peer said those words and proceeded to tell me that I would fail at the promotion I recently earned. Our past, events, and people in our lives, even if just for a little while, all contribute to who we are. Some people take the "victim mentality" ("I am this way because of *fill in the blank*."). Or, like me, they don't even realize how much something impacted them. I do know I was deeply hurt by what my coworker said. I shared it with my boss at the time. Her response: "She didn't mean anything by it, move on." Internally, I thought maybe I was making a big deal out of nothing and tried to forget about it. It didn't work.

As life progressed, I overcompensated by doing everything. If I did everything, I thought I'd be seen as smart and competent. As I got older, it became a matter of my self-worth. I had to know everything; and, let's not forget, I was telling everyone I knew that I knew everything! I did not realize at the time that by working so hard to show everyone I was smart and deserved to be in the roles I was in, I was inadvertently pushing everyone away—people I worked with, friends, and family. This is regression, not growth.

In 2015, due to a job change, I had the opportunity to rethink everything. It was the scariest time of my life. Little did I know, it would be the best thing for me.

For decades leading up to this opportunity, I felt stuck in a box. I would wake up early, go to work, come home late, go to bed, then do it all over again the next day. It kept getting worse. I went from working forty-five to fifty hours a week to working seventy or more hours with no end in sight. This included a lot of traveling and working weeks without a day off. Needless to say, I hit a brick wall. There was no creativity, new ideas, or innovation happening for me, either personally or professionally.

It was time for me to step back and figure out who I was and *what I wanted out of each day*! Time to stop waking up for someone else's reason to get out of bed. I created a new "why" for myself:

I get out of bed every morning to remind those I interact with: They are better than they think they are, and can do more than they think they can!

My "why" grounds me in everything I do. I finally realized I am good enough, and I can do more than I ever gave myself credit for. I finally believed in myself!

I had my *why*, so I was all set…well, not quite. I still had to become self-aware. *95 percent of people think they are self-aware; in reality, less than 15 percent are truly self-aware.* Based on research by Tasha Eurich in 2017:

I was *definitely* part of the 95 percent.

I did believe in myself, but that didn't change my desire to let everyone know I was good enough. Looking back, it was like a pendulum; I swung from one side all the way to the other without stopping in the middle. Self-awareness means you are aware of, and truly care about, how your actions affect those around you.

In 2017, a powerful behavioral assessment tool transformed my level of self-awareness. It helped me understand my natural abilities and that my self-awareness would grow if I embraced them. The assessment provides an understanding of one's needs and why they sometimes do what they do. The hard work comes in choosing to do something with that knowledge. I had been exposed to a variety of behavioral assessments over the years, but this was very different. The assessment allowed me to understand what my needs were and why I behaved in certain ways to fulfill those needs. Over the next year or two I really embraced this newfound self-understanding. I felt as if all the puzzle pieces were coming together.

It only took me forty years to get there...so don't give up!

To me, growth is about bringing your best self to each day in everything you do. Is a promotion at work growth? Maybe, in my opinion, it depends on your path to the promotion. For some, growth could mean gaining knowledge; maybe it's a college degree or certifications. What if it's forced on you? I have known parents who told their kids, "No matter what, you are going to college." Does college mean growth? Maybe to some. Can growth be forced?

If you're comfortable, you're most likely not growing. Think about the last time you were uncomfortable. It's easier—and let's be real, less scary—to stay comfortable. Comfortable can also mean complacent.

My story is one of the many incredible examples of growth in this book. At the end of the day, growth can mean something different to everyone. We are all unique, which makes each of us wonderful—not right, wrong, or even different. Just wonderful!

I leave you with this thought: *be aware.* Everything you do influences those you interact with every day. Are you encouraging those you influence to bring their best self to each day? Are you creating a space of grace and respect, both personally and professionally? When someone gives you feedback, try your best to look at the feedback as a gift, not an insult, even if they are not coming from the best place when giving that feedback.

We can't control anyone else. We only have the power to choose our response to what someone says or does. This concept comes from Viktor Frankl, an Austrian neurologist, psychiatrist, philosopher, writer, and Holocaust survivor. When imprisoned in the death camps of Nazi

Germany, he experienced horrific things, including seeing his parents, brother, and wife all sent to the gas ovens. One day, he became aware of what he later called "the last of the human freedoms." His captors could control his environment, what they did to him and to those around him, but they could not control how he let their actions affect him. Between what happens to us, or the stimulus, and our response to it, is the freedom or power to choose that response.

We have all had situations where we wish we could have a magical "do-over." I don't have the power to change the past, but I can own my future. It's not easy. Every day I remind myself why I get out of bed in the morning, and I give my all to everyone and everything. Do I make mistakes? Heck yeah! But when I go to bed at night, I take a few minutes to think through my day and assess how I did:

- *Did I own my actions?*
- *Did I pause before responding to someone or a situation?*
- *Did I bring my best self to the day?*

If I answer "yes" to all those questions, I go to bed with a smile. If there is a "no," I own it and quickly decide how tomorrow will be better. That's my growth…what's yours?

Kimberly Vissak is one of those lucky people who, for over twenty-five years, has been able to do what she loves. As Chief Learning Officer of Build A Team Consultants, her passion is to help enhance leaders' ability to recruit, hire, develop, and maintain top talent to ensure business results are maximized.

Kimberly's leadership career began in the early '90s, followed by a focus on learning, development, and human resource management in 2000. This is where she became passionate about servant leadership and developed her talents through certification in The Ken Blanchard Companies and Franklin Covey leadership programs. Most recently, she partnered with Perspective Consulting LLC, a Predictive Index Certified Partner where she received her Talent Optimization Certification to help empower business leaders to design winning teams.

She looks forward to continuing to help others reach their full potential.

kimberly@buildateamconsultants.com
www.linkedin.com/in/kimberly-vissak

Gabrielle Cole

I Have Something to Say

Graduating from undergrad in 2011 was a great time. I was ready to take on the world. My plan was to get a part-time job in any field to make a living, preferably a law clerk, while I studied law back home in Saint Louis. This was my entire thought process while driving back home from Chicago. People back home always told me, "You may not get to be and do all the things you want to in your life," or "Life is never a perfect plan, so just go with the flow," or "I always wanted to do things in my career, but life got in the way." Well, I listened, respectfully, and then did what I felt in my heart to fulfill my passions. At that time, I was twenty-one: no home, no children, no debt, and just trying to understand who I was becoming— what I wanted to become. Planting seeds to be a rock star attorney, one day a judge, and a philanthropist dedicated to serving women and children. I had it all figured out. I can plan my life out perfectly so that when there's a bump in the journey, I can navigate with ease.

Then, my journey shifted.

That journey started with service. As I was doing community service by volunteering for local hunger relief organizations, I realized something new: there are people in this world who literally have no food, and the food we were distributing was not sufficient. It was devastating. In addition to the politics and traditional structure of applying to law school,

119

I started to doubt my passion for justice, in relation to our legal system, in addition to our society's idea of what justice means, and what that meant to me. I reflected. But maybe it was not a reflection; maybe it was a change of heart?

I wrapped up the law school process and later completed my master's degree in Nonprofit Management with ease and satisfaction. I talked with families in inner-city communities, started to understand the issues beneath the surface, and made a connection with the people. I had officially grown into a person who realized it was not about the things I wanted out of life, for my life, but the importance of life for humanity. I often wonder, "Will there always be a need for food pantries, or shelter, or aid of any kind? And if so, can we work as a People to help one another?" This is what justice meant to me at this point in life. I wanted to unite and support people for collective growth and sustainability in our local communities for the children. That is my meaning of justice.

All grown up now, I know that there are more seeds to plant—in my children, in my family, my colleagues, my students, my friends, in *me*. Juggling life is a concept, and I choose good ethics, community leadership, love, peace, and becoming a wife and mother as one part of my journey. On the other hand, managing family dynamics, financial instability due to medical bills and educational debt, walking away from politics, experiencing difficult people, and witnessing suffering have all brought my experience full circle. The combination of passion and daily struggle was the way of my personal development. It was growth. I now have something to say, with warmth, confidence, and authenticity. My truth and my experience! I remember asking myself, "Why do I get emotionally invested in other people's words and actions?"

It is because I care. I want humanity to thrive and uplift each other, though that's out of my control. To share my words, I must stay true to myself and my experience. I can acknowledge what others say or do, and then let it go. The practice of "letting go" is a major part of my journey to continuously serve others, be genuine, and speak my truth.

I needed boundaries. I met with a planning coach to help me set myself up for success. My definition of success now is the ability to help the community in various capacities, be with my family, personally develop, all while sharing my experience and knowledge with others. From my perspective, growth is ongoing, so success today will mean something different in the future. I came to realize that in a world so loud, all I wanted was to quiet my overthinking, over-planning mind, and just be over it all. Speaking with another individual helped me clear my thoughts for a vision of the comfortable life I wanted now. I started with listing out realities and my dreams and making the connections. Four themes emerged: Time Management, Family, Enjoyment, and *Growth*. One exercise that made the most impact was developing a set of personal and leadership commandments. I had to put my values, thoughts, and whatever else that was important to me on paper and into writing.

The goal was to live by these commandments. My moral development and planning exercise turned into rigorous self-care routines and setting boundaries I needed so badly. I do not have the perfect schedule or the perfect finances. Sometimes I get absolutely nothing complete in a day, but that is OK. I have set standards that are realistic and good for my health. I may not accomplish all my goals at once or in a year. However, the action items and boundaries will help me get closer to that ideal situation.

My most important action items are:

8. Start reading again! I feed my mind with books, research, and articles on a variety of topics throughout the year.

9. Pick one day weekly to spend two hours on self-care. Self-care can be going on a nature walk, journaling, spa day at home or in a spa, anything for me! (I like this one.) I also enjoy the traditional

practice of hot yoga, as it really clears my mind and body. I am realizing that putting these workouts on my calendar is vital to staying committed and ensuring I am taking care of myself!

10. Every Sunday, set up my week with reflection, priorities, and calendar management. I spend most of that time accepting or declining meetings put on my schedule during inappropriate times. For instance, one of my boundaries is blocking work time that is not for meetings. Another boundary is allowing my schedule for no more than two evening meetings per week so I can be with my young kids.

Overall, I had ten commandments for myself that included boundaries, three focus goals with numerous action items, and, lastly, someone or two to confide in for moral support.

I want you to ask yourself, "What is it that I want to do?" Then do it! Be realistic, remember what matters most, and give yourself room to grow and give yourself grace!

Here's an exercise you might like to try that really helped me clarify my boundaries. Schedule some time to be alone for the day. Journal about some situations in your life that are not working for you, then create a boundary and an action item to go alongside each conflict. Write as many as you want, but at least three. Then think about what self-care means for you, review your calendar, and make some hard decisions to include at least one two-hour block of time for self-care. We cannot take care of others if we are not taken care of first. Yes, that is a true statement. Then get started! Set some sort of timeline to your action items.

My Example

Identify the conflict:
- My calendar is full of meetings with no time for anything else.

Action items:
- Combine all calendars to get an overview of all my weeks.

- Schedule weekly standing meetings.
- Put work blocks on external or shared calendars so people know in real time when I'm available/free.

Set Boundary:
- No more than two evening meetings a week.
- Start to schedule meetings on Monday–Wednesday, with little flexibility for meetings on Thursday and Fridays. This way I can write, create deliverables, and work on collateral materials. (This is an action item too.)

This is a starting point that can take you a long way. Remember, find a buddy. Journaling is amazing, but sometimes it is helpful to have a trustworthy work friend to plan and share ideas with, or a super fun girlfriend to decompress with over early dinner. It's all a part of growing.

When we hear the word "growth," we think major moves, world-class accomplishments, or stellar career advancements. These are possible meanings for growth, but for me it is the process of learning with an open mind, evolving with care, and leading with grace. I have various tangible accomplishments to show from my growth, but for me growth is a process that is interchangeable and looks different for each of us. Through my community work and new understanding of justice, daily life dynamics of being a mother and being in a long-term relationship, and getting myself through other traumatic life complications, I am still here, stronger than yesterday, living in my truth. Well, that's all for now... Time will only tell for us all what the next chapter of our own personal growth will encompass.

Gabi Cole is a nonprofit executive, resource development consultant, and adjunct professor. Born and raised in North St. Louis City, Missouri, she studied political science and sociology at DePaul University, then obtained a Master of Science in Non-Profit Management from Fontbonne University.

Her passion for human services and overall wellness drove her to research and develop a local wellness nonprofit program established in 2012 for underserved families in the St. Louis area. Gabi has exceptional leadership experience with racial equity work, creating and leading successful programs, direct practice with vulnerable families, public relations, and organizational planning. Her honesty as a community health leader, great educator, and professional work has humbled her viewpoint in working with at-risk communities.

She believes that social and community organizations should be mission-driven and stay true to their values. Gabi is a member of the American Public Health Association and has been recognized for several outstanding leadership and fundraising awards. Gabi is married with two children and resides in North Saint Louis City.

gcole.my.canva.site/
www.facebook.com/gabrielle.moorecarter/
www.linkedin.com/in/gabrielle-cole-mnm-30738138/

Mary Brice

To Choose Growth Again and Again

For me, growth happened while I was busy trying to achieve other things.

When I was a senior in college, we philosophy majors took a series of exams covering all four years of our coursework in that subject. The day after the exams, the department head called me into his office to tell me that I had gotten the highest score in the class, so he was "adjusting" the scores of the young man with the second highest results. He didn't think that the only female student in the department should have the top ranking.

I was too stunned to say anything. I didn't feel then that I could take action to change my situation—but it fueled my determination to try.

But by the time I was in the English Literature PhD program at Notre Dame, I had grown much stronger.

After getting a C on my first paper in the doctoral program, I met with the department chair to ask for his advice. I never got a grade below A again. (He did say my paper "sounded like a philosophy major wrote it." There may have been some truth to that.)

Only 33 percent of those accepted into a humanities doctoral program complete the PhD. Finishing is certainly not a matter of intelligence—most of my classmates were smarter, and some were conspicuously gifted. Completing the degree is purely a matter of perseverance.

When my dissertation committee demanded a ninth round of revisions, I really didn't know if I had it in me. But I remember deciding that, if they wanted me to quit, they would have to come to my office and snap all my pens in half by hand. In the end, the committee considered my work so strong that they waived the defense requirement. (At least that was their story. I've always suspected that I just wore them down.)

After $40,000 and two hard years of an MBA program, my first job interview ended with being told that I wasn't "quantitative enough to be hired." I sought out my statistics professor for advice, revised my interview strategy, and earned the only brand management job offer in my class.

Clearly, I believed that the answer to all problems was to try harder. To study harder. To work harder. And perseverance *is* a great strategy. It's the solution to a multitude of problems and something I wish for my own daughter.

And yet.

In my early years, I had little interest in growth. Growth seemed so slow, so passive, so not-run-by-me. But growth happened anyway when I wasn't looking. I hadn't just grown stronger. I had become calmer, less prickly, more patient, more tolerant.

I began wondering, "What if growth isn't as passive a process as I have always thought? What if I could bring to growth the same energy and purpose I have relied on to manage setbacks with exams, papers, and job interviews?"

Could I take an intentional approach to growth?

I don't know if I'm doing growth right. But I do know there are things we can do to encourage growth—to invite it into our lives, to foster it, and even to hasten it. We do this by adding intentionality, by making deliberate choices, in at least these four ways:

Open All the Gifts

Everything that happens in our lives really is an opportunity—to learn something, to connect with someone, to grow. But I've discovered that I must actively *look* for the meaning, to deliberately pursue the insight, to open my mind and my heart to what I'm supposed to be learning. I must open the gift if I want to receive anything.

This is especially true of the failures, the frustrations, the mild aggravations.

At first these gifts appear unappealing—the socks and underwear of the universe—the gifts I don't want but really need. I've learned to open them anyway.

It's only a gift if you open it. Otherwise, it's just a box.

Don't Just Embrace the Growth Cycle—Kickstart It

Perseverance is linear—we move *forward*, and *toward* our goals. But growth is round. It's a cycle.

I read somewhere that growth is the result of completing a challenge cycle, in which we go through distinct stages, first feeling frightened, then excited, then challenged, satisfied, coasting, bored, cranky, itchy.

(OK, I added that last one.)

We sometimes hear people say, after finally reaching their goals, they feel a sense of letdown. This seems natural. The cycle itself has caused them to grow, and they can no longer be comfortable where they are.

We can deliberately propel this cycle forward. We can learn to recognize when we're in the "satisfied" stage and begin then to plan for the next challenge.

We can be intentional about repeating this cycle. We can always be starting something new. Always planning what to learn next. Even though it will mean always being frightened (and sometimes terrified) of whatever new adventure we're starting.

To begin the cycle again, I have to accept the frightened stage. Because that's where the cycle begins. So, I hope to choose to always be terrified about some aspect of my life.

Why would I leave a perfectly good comfort zone? Because the itchiness means my cocoon is too tight.

If You Can't Find a Mentor, Make One

All of us want mentors—women who help guide us as we grow. But many women say they can't find them.

LinkedIn surveys, *Forbes* magazine articles, blog posts by the Society for Human Resource Management, a study by HR consulting firm Development Dimensions International—all report that there are many more women looking for mentors than there are successful women willing to mentor them. How, then, can we find the guidance, the inspiration, and the example that we need to grow?

If we can't find off-the-shelf mentors, we have to make our own. We build them using aspects of every woman with a strength, a stellar quality, or a good habit we would like to have. We can energetically plagiarize every winning attitude and copy every success behavior. There is no patent protection for character.

Start by identifying eight or ten areas in which you wish you had guidance. Areas like leadership, self-discipline, kindness, generosity, discretion, lifelong learning. Then make a deliberate effort to piece together your own mentor, proactively searching for women with strengths in the areas in which you want to grow.

We already know women we admire. What if we didn't stop at admiration? Instead, intentionally add those aspects you admire to the mentor you are creating:

- How to say "no" graciously.
- How to admit a mistake.

- How to deflect criticism calmly.

- When to ask for help and when to tough it out.

- How to behave at a meeting, offer constructive criticism, defuse tension with humor.

Someone you know is good at all these things.

Don't be blinded by the fact that this someone may be younger than you—or older, less experienced, less well-paid, less educated, or even that she wears outfits you hate. You are building your own mentor, and you can't let surface issues distract you from recognizing what may be the perfect example of a quality you need.

Copy the strengths you admire and the qualities that impress you and leave the rest. Whatever is less than perfect is part of *her* growth journey, not yours.

By Frequent Anguish

I don't know how old you are. I don't know where you're from. I may not even know your name.

Yet I know—with absolute certainty—one of the most intimate truths about you. I know you've had your heart broken.

The specifics don't matter. For me it was a very sad childhood (alcoholism—you know the rest). For everyone, it's something. The death of a child, a sibling, a parent—by cancer, overdose, even suicide. A bitter divorce, a horrific accident, a terrible diagnosis—crushing losses of all kinds. No one escapes heartbreak.

Everyone has lost something.

The advanced degrees and the professional successes, the goals, and the challenges. Those experiences built skills, and I'm grateful for every skill I've gained. But growth came less from gains than from losses.

It has been from sorrows that I've grown the most, and maybe that's true for you too.

Heartbreak changed how I saw others. No matter how accomplished or organized or educated or well dressed, everyone is broken—maybe even bleeding—on the inside. Knowing that—really seeing it—has made me more compassionate, more patient, and (strangely) more cheerful. It has left me with a strong sense of connection to others and of community that successes, for all their rewards, never did.

I came, over time, to understand that sorrow is not a contest. It's a constant. And heartbreak is not a competition. It *is* the level playing field.

I don't know that anyone can actively welcome sorrow, but I can be open, given time, to the growth that loss surprises me with.

If growth is something we can encourage with intentionality, how, then, can we know we are succeeding? Without the achievements and goals, the traditional measures of success? Without the classmates, male or female, to be ranked against?

By the only metric that matters: how far we've come.

Mary Brice helps university researchers to commercialize their innovations by guiding them through customer discovery, value proposition design, financial forecasting, and capital investment planning.

Mary has coached over two hundred ventures and is a frequent speaker on launching and scaling successful start-ups. She contributes a monthly column on innovation commercialization to *Elixir*, the St. Louis University publication for faculty researchers.

She is an active investor in three angel groups and a member of the St. Louis Arch Angels Board of Directors.

She served as Board Chair of Gateway Venture Mentoring Service, an MIT-created, nonprofit entrepreneur coaching program, where she wrote the organization's business plan.

Mary earned a PhD in English from the University of Notre Dame and an MBA from Emory University.

She has served as the director of the MBA program at Hamline University and as an adjunct professor of New Products and Marketing at the University of St. Thomas.

marybrice2@gmail.com
www.linkedin.com/in/marybricephd/
314-719-9826

Audra Harrold

Fashionably Horsin' Around

April 10, 2020. The day I lost my job. I was working in the fashion industry for a nonprofit, managing local designer programs, educational programming, and fashion events. I was a single mom to two teenage boys, and had three dogs and a mortgage. Little did the nonprofit—nor a pandemic or, most importantly, me—know at the time that losing my job was one of the biggest gifts in my life.

So, how did a girl growing up in Seattle who loved spending her days with filthy fingernails and the smell of horses end up in the fashion world?

I've always been a horse girl. It's in my blood and who I am. Yet being raised by a single mom, having horses was never in the budget. But, true to my nature, I found clever ways to be around horses. In high school, my best girlfriend and I would clean stalls, polish tack, pick pastures, and camp in haylofts overnight, keeping watch over mares ready to foal, all for a chance to hear those words: "Would you like to ride?"

I wore hand-me-down show clothes that didn't fit and rode horses who were green broke. While other riders confidently trotted in wearing their tailored jackets atop their expensive and well-trained mounts, I was happy to make it past the spooky ingate and into the arena as my wide-eyed horse jumped a little sideways. But I didn't notice or care about those other riders. I was doing something I loved with pride. Then something I didn't expect happened. For my sixteenth birthday, instead of the hundreds of horse-power most teenagers want, I was gifted the only horsepower I ever wished for. Horsepower of *one*. A horse of my own. I was an equestrian.

As I transitioned from teenager to college student, then to young adult and to married woman with two young boys, horses, confidence, passion, and being scrappy consistently became a part of my story.

In 2009, I moved from Eastern North Carolina to St. Louis with a husband, two boxer dogs, two young boys, and a horse. Life was good. I was raising two wonderful boys in a new city, making friends, enjoying the foodie scene, and riding. With my newer "mom body," I found that my riding clothes didn't fit like they used to, and no matter how I adjusted my sizing they still didn't fit right. I found myself tugging on my clothes as I was cantering around on a twelve-hundred-pound animal instead of focusing on what we were working on. Not a good combination when atop a live animal with a mind of its own. I started to note the things that frustrated me about my riding clothes. When I couldn't find the perfect fit, I decided I would figure out how to make the fit perfect for me and other equestrians facing the same problem.

And just like that, I started my journey into the world of fashion.

I entered the industry with the bright-eyed naivete of a kindergartner on her first day of school. I believed everything everyone said and was drawn into the intoxicating world of shiny-thing promises. I was unaware of the wolves circling around me calculating their messaging so I would continue to go down the rainbow path they paved. What I couldn't see, or maybe didn't want to see, was the path was full of potholes and cracks, which became more costly with each step. I was blinded by promises of *Today Show* appearances and celebrity endorsements of my equestrian line of sport clothing. I dipped deeply into my savings to pay for services that didn't deliver and that I didn't need. I hired an expensive consultant to help me navigate the unknown world I was in. I was flying to New York City on a regular basis because if I didn't manufacture in the capital city of fashion, then I wouldn't be taken seriously, right? I had an expensive, fancy website with features and buttons I didn't need. I was caught up in a tidal wave of believing the wrong things and trusting the wrong people.

I spent thousands of dollars on inventory to sell online and take with me to horse shows. While the brand was created for female riders like me, I found that the brand messaging was attractive to a younger audience. I decided to create apparel for younger riders. More fabric, more samples, more trips, more, more, more. I dipped deeper into my savings, determined to make this work. In my attempt to create another sales channel, I was instead creating a bigger challenge. I was sucked up in a whirling funnel cloud, spinning out of control with no way out but to jump.

The spending had to stop. Something had to change. I slammed on the brakes to regroup. I hosted a pop-up liquidation event to sell off excess inventory that was piling up in my basement. During this event, a woman showed up and asked a lot of questions. I questioned her motives, suspicious that perhaps she was a spy gearing up to launch a competitor. The truth, as it turned out, was she had purchased a small batch apparel manufacturing facility that included equestrian show clothing patterns. The equestrian industry was something she knew nothing about, but I did. After careful (or so I thought) vetting of the situation and her, I decided to jump in and form a new partnership. I shipped all my fabrics from NYC to STL and started manufacturing the line in St. Louis.

Unfortunately, as much due diligence as I did, I missed the mark… by a long shot. My biggest fears of production being sidelined for other clients came true. The manufacturing quality was riddled with mistakes, my business partner was a terrible businesswoman, and the production facility was on a sharp downslide straight into a business graveyard.

While all of this was going on, I committed to increasing my knowledge base of the business. Backward and forward. Inside and out. I wasn't traditionally trained in a fashion program, so I knew my learning curve was going to be steep. Yet I was hungry, determined, and, most importantly, I loved the industry and the people in it. I learned a lot, and I met people who proved to be essential in my journey. I met designers and product development specialists, technical designers, seamstresses, fabric reps, models, photographers, factory owners, organizations—the list goes on. I picked their brains and sat by their sides. I sat in on approval meetings and quickly learned the top challenges of the industry. I dove headfirst into the learning pool and completely submerged myself as I grew as a professional in a new industry.

I came to really see the mistakes I had made. I spent money—a lot of money—on a PR firm I didn't need. I purchased yards and yards of fabrics, made sample after sample, and overproduced my inventory. My business mind knew all of this was wrong, but the sheep surrounding me (clearly in disguise) were so convincing that it was only when I looked back that I realized I had been taken advantage of. It took putting on my big-girl panties to acknowledge the mistakes, swallow the losses, and refocus on the growth and new opportunity these mistakes were providing.

As I was deconstructing and reconstructing my journey, I took a solid look back at that first meeting in that unsuspecting wolf den with a whole new perspective and appreciation. I was able to acknowledge that *all* of this was supposed to happen. I had to walk this journey so I could legitimately shoot up warning flares for other fashion professionals because I had been there.

My redefined path and the root of my passion now is to provide resources, support, and opportunity (sprinkled with some brilliant advice combined with some pushing and prodding) to aspiring, emerging, and established fashion professionals to keep them on a path to success.

Had I not made those mistakes with my equestrian line, I wouldn't be able to organically connect with the people I support. Today, I work with fashion professionals and love every minute of it. I am the cofounder and executive director of STL Fashion Alliance, which is a nonprofit dedicated to local fashion professionals. I provide connections and mentorships, educational resources, and grant opportunities. I also listen, I guide, I care, and I show up. If my equestrian business hadn't failed, and if I hadn't lost my job in April 2020, I wouldn't have the experience and street cred to do what I do.

Who knew a young girl scrapping a riding outfit together would end up landing in an industry where the clothing is made? Opportunity is in everything and is everywhere. Sometimes opportunities are clear and right in front of us, and sometimes we are turned upside down and dropped on our heads before we can see it. Identify the pieces that add to your story and continue to grow. I keep adding every day.

Audra Harrold is the Cofounder and Executive Director of STL Fashion Alliance. Her passion focuses on providing connection, resources, and support for aspiring, emerging, and established fashion professionals in all categories within the industry. Her nontraditional entrance into the fashion world started as a solution to a problem when she was riding competitive horses.

She volunteers on numerous boards, including Fashion Group International St. Louis Chapter and Lindenwood University Fashion Business & Design Advisory Council. She also serves as a mentor to high school groups.

Originally from Seattle, Audra earned her BA in Communications from the University of Washington and attended postgraduate art school studying commercial photography. She has lived on the West Coast, the East Coast, and is now currently in the Midwest where she is raising her two sons and a house full of dogs (both residents and fosters). She is working on a global tech solution for fashion industry connections.

www.linkedin.com/in/audra-harrold-37856448
www.stlfashionalliance.org

Rebecca Fehlig

You Can't Stay Here

As the big 5-0 looms this year, I reflect on the first half of my life in milestones, not years. The college me naively thought life's best experiences happened in a certain order, and all by age 25. I clearly watched too many Friends episodes. Eventually and fortunately, I learned otherwise. There are my "Baltimore 20s," filled with firsts, like my first time living outside St. Louis, first mortgage, first daughter, and my first marriage (yes, in that order.) Then I moved to Boise, Idaho (an attempt to escape my problems, which I also learned never works.) This move was a breaking point, and I decided to end my marriage. By my early 30s, I lived my "getting-my-act-together" years by single parenting, attending graduate school, and launching a new and meaningful career. My 40s have been defined by abundance. In the last 10 years, I found and married my true love, became a proud St. Louis city resident, dove into international travel, experienced career growth, and expanded my beautiful and motley crew. Along the way, I have learned that I make better choices when I validate my needs as being as relevant as someone else's, and when I resist the urge to fix or change someone (cue the Serenity Prayer.) Sounds obvious, right? For some reason, it took writing this chapter to acknowledge this, and may take even longer to fully understand why.

I was two years old when women finally gained the legal right to have a credit card without their husband's signature, thanks to the Equal Credit Opportunity Act. My mom told me that it was not uncommon for women to attend college for the sole purpose of finding a husband (attaining their "Mrs." degree.) She graduated with a B.A. and joked that marrying in her early 20s was considered 'old' by some. Women were starting to find their voice and realize their right to make their own health care decisions. I now see how my grandparents treated their daughters and sons differently… both with love, but there was no question as to which gender was given deference. My mom's advice on relationships and career was always one of encouragement and empowerment. She may have been living vicariously through my sister and me. During the years her identity was being shaped, laws were in place that did not see her gender as equal. Because I went to college, played sports, and supported myself financially, I thought I was immune from the impact of the biases of my parents' generation. This was not true. We all carry the norms of the prior generation to some extent. My first marriage is an example of the dangers of putting someone else's needs before my own, but also thinking it is my responsibility to change someone.

"You can't stay here," I said. My daughter was in second grade and I was standing in my kitchen when I gave the person on the other end of the phone the number for a nearby homeless shelter. This person was calling me because they had no money, no friends or family in town, and had nowhere to sleep that night. They asked to stay in my apartment because they had no other options. This person was my first husband and saying no to rescuing him that night was a turning point. His needs routinely came before my daughter's and mine. That night, they didn't. In that moment, I knew I could never change or fix him, nor was it my responsibility. My job was to put my daughter's needs first, which also meant prioritizing mine.

It wasn't easy. I struggled with feelings of guilt and sadness, but sometimes moving forward means walking away from the past.

My first marriage offered countless opportunities to for me to leave. I attended Al-Anon meetings and saw other people share a future I feared. We went to couple's therapy and were reminded the goal of our sessions was not to stay married, but to find happiness. We experienced financial strain from his constant job losses and emotional strain from all the times he just didn't come home. I finally left.

After I filed for divorce, the getting-my-act-together years gained momentum. I sought a career that could pay the mortgage, but also aligned with my values. I chose a career in nonprofit, and I've never looked back. I went to graduate school and then was hired by Autism Speaks. Through incredible bosses, mentors, and the devotion of my parents to help care for my daughter on weekends, late nights, and work trips, I took on more and more responsibility and ultimately moved into national leadership roles in two large and impactful health nonprofits.

At the same time, I began to fuel my desire to experience different cultures. Through International Volunteer Headquarters, my kids (foreshadowing) and I volunteered and lived with families in Central, South America, and South Africa. Recently, I joined Meds & Food for Kids (an amazing nonprofit) on a trip to Haiti to experience their mission and the profound resilience of Haitians firsthand. In retrospect, these years were critical to what was next. I found fulfillment and confidence by exploring my passions. And that's when it happened. "Right in the middle of an ordinary life, love brings you a fairy tale." (Verbiage on a candle holder in my windowsill as a gift from my former boss.)

I Googled, "Is love at first sight real?" after our first encounter. He brought two beautiful little ones to the mix and my journey into abundance took off. Blending our families gave each of us what we wanted—a loving, equal and respectful partner, and more children to raise and love. We had a shared understanding of single parenting, and soon shared disdain for of the term "step." We both came into our marriages with full legal and physical custody of our children due to mental health or addiction issues from our former spouses. We had and still have the full responsibility (and all the joys and tears that come with that) of raising our three children. Our family has different last names, and the children share no DNA, but blood makes you related, love (and some quirky family traditions and humor) makes you a family. Although madly in love, it broke my heart when I experienced how abandonment harms a child. My son was abandoned by his biological parents as a newborn, and then again by his adoptive mother. This had a profound effect on his self, his worldview, our how our family blended and, at times, didn't. At its worst, I tried to fix him and help our family. I took a leave from my job and our family of five moved to Puerto Rico for a summer to surround him with love, support, and potentially beneficial therapies. This approach didn't work, and finally an attachment expert, Shirley Crenshaw, helped us adapt our parenting and his environment so he could feel secure. This was difficult and counter intuitive, but life-changing for our family.

The last couple years have marked a time of transition and loss. Lyla left home for college, Sasha enlisted in the U.S. Navy, my sister and her family moved away, and our beloved family dog, Nacho Pancho Bob, died.

But the loss that has left a permanent mark on me was my mom's sudden death. By the time she had a diagnosis, there weren't any hopeful treatment options. Pandemic restrictions prevented us from seeing her until her last few days. The lack of control I felt during her illness and death was profound and maddening. In fact, I haven't really shaken that anger or the pain of that loss.

So, what's next? I need to appreciate and acknowledge my past, my privilege, and my learnings. I think back to the woman on the phone with her ex-husband who felt guilt, angst, and the deep desire to rescue, and want to tell her I am proud of her. She resisted these engrained responses and chose her and her daughter's futures. I want to hug the woman who felt desperate when she was trying to help her son and let her know he will be okay. I want to tell her all the "mistakes" she made in life were necessary in becoming the parent, colleague, wife, aunt, neighbor, friend, volunteer, sister, and boss she is today. And I hope I bring those learnings and forgiveness to my future self, as I know I will continue to stumble, learn, and grieve along the way.

Although grit played a role in my life lessons, I also had an advantage growing up as a white cis-gendered female surrounded by people who believed in me, a community that was well resourced and looked like me, and lived among systems that were built to provide opportunities for people like me. This acknowledgment shapes what is next for me.

Although my mom's tendency to put others before herself was passed on to me, so were her purposeful and intentional choices in life. She never measured success by income or title. These may not have felt attainable to her, but she always pursued personal growth. In reflection, I guess I have, too. With that (and her) as my guide, I can't wait to see what's in store.

Rebecca Fehlig worked in the print industry in Baltimore, Boise, and St. Louis for 10 years after graduating from Truman State University. Her interest in having positive impact in the lives of others led her to graduate school at Washington University followed by a career in nonprofit. Thanks to amazing mentors, she has had local and national roles at both Autism Speaks and the National MS Society. She currently serves the mission of the MS Society as its EVP of Operations where she leads a large and talented team across the country.

As a recent graduate of Focus Leadership St. Louis, she's reinvigorated to invest more in her community. A few organizations she currently supports are Meds & Food for Kids, United Way, Nerinx Hall, and Forward Through Ferguson. With two of her three children "launched," she's eager to spend any spare time running and traveling.

You can contact Rebecca at:
www.linkedin.com/in/rfehlig/

Brooke Sieb

Balance and Boundaries

During a time of personal and professional chaos, I received one of the scariest phone calls of my life. I was traveling for work during a stressful project when my husband called. "Elliott is fine, but we are in the hospital. She woke up in the middle of the night, and as I was holding her she had a seizure. I called 911, and an ambulance took us to the hospital." The world stopped, and I couldn't breathe. Our daughter, Elliott, was only a year-and-a-half old with no previous medical issues. I immediately searched for flights home. The earliest flight arrived in the afternoon, so all I could do was sit and wait. When I finally got to the hospital, I found my daughter in a dark room, in a crib hooked with wires everywhere. After testing, she received a common diagnosis for small children (seizures triggered by fever), and we hoped she would grow out of it.

I'd never felt such guilt. On one hand, I loved my work and felt I had a responsibility to my company and team. On the other hand, I was barely present for my family right before Elliott's seizure. The company I worked for at the time was implementing the largest system conversion they'd ever undertaken. I told myself I needed to work harder to get the project accomplished and then I would be home more. I had no concept of a healthy work-life balance at this point in my career.

By March 2020, my responsibilities at work had markedly increased by this time, and then the pandemic hit. As an essential employee, I was focused on developing new processes to ensure that our business could continue to operate with no disruption in client service. I'm proud to say we accomplished that, but I will also say, not proudly, that I didn't use the opportunity to slow down and enjoy life like many people did. I was working a lot, but, ultimately, I was not doing my best work because I never had a chance to recharge. I wasn't the best version of myself for my family, either, for the same reason. I lacked patience, energy, and focus.

In May of 2021, I took my first real vacation as a parent where I was fully unplugged and truly present. Sure, traveling with children is stressful, but not allowing the mental stress of my inbox to creep in was freeing. My team handled the fire drills that arose at work, and gave me much needed time away after a very stressful 2020. I'll forever be grateful to them. After I got home, I was not the same person. Those slow mornings on the beach, drinking coffee and playing with my kids, made me realize I was not happy living the way I had been. My perspective changed.

I started to leave work on time more often. I wasn't overly anxious if I didn't make it to the office before eight a.m. I made sure to do my job to the best of my ability but prioritized my tasks. I didn't treat everything as a four-alarm fire. "What if there is an issue? What if they need me?" These were regular thoughts I had in the past. I was so wrapped up in that mindset that I genuinely thought I was indispensable to the business. (I laugh about that now.) Slowly but surely, I began to realize I needed a full paradigm shift.

Fast-forward to August 24, 2021, when I received the second scariest phone call of my life. My husband had picked Elliott up from daycare; she was having another seizure, and this one was different. She didn't have a fever and it happened out of the blue. They were in an ambulance on the way to the hospital. When I arrived, I was informed that Elliott had a second seizure in the ambulance. She had to be intubated and placed on a ventilator to protect her airway. Nothing in my life prepared me for seeing my daughter in that state. In those moments in the hospital, I realized how fragile life is. How lucky have I been to be blessed with good health my entire life? How fortunate am I that my grade-school-aged son Nolan barely catches a cold? My heart ached for people who deal with hospital stays, dosage amounts, and testing every single day.

In September 2021, I decided it was time to make a change. A dear friend once told me, "When the bad days outweigh the good days in any area of your life, you've got to pay attention." I took a hard look at what I was doing and couldn't answer the question "Why?" anymore. I needed to find the right balance between my personal and professional lives. I gave my notice in mid-October and took a hybrid position that allowed me to work from home three days a week. It was a game changer. I was in a healthy work environment and encouraged to take care of myself and my family first with no fear of repercussions. I could help get my children ready for the day and be home when my son got off the school bus. This was the first time in my life I've been able to do that guilt-free.

In March of 2022, my husband and I took time off work to take Nolan on a spring break trip. Nolan carries some stress with having a little sister who has seizures, so it was good for him to get away and be a carefree kid for a week. This also meant that Elliott got to enjoy some one-on-one time with one of her favorite people, her grandmother. We had an amazing time together exploring, going out to eat, swimming, and just being present in the moment. While I was away, no one contacted me. And guess what? Everyone survived and I was still a valued member of the team when I returned.

Three days after we returned home, Elliott had her third seizure. This time I was with her when she started seizing. I held her with one arm and dialed 911 with the other, while my husband administered her medication. It was a full-circle moment. I realized I still had guilt for not being there for her when she had her first two seizures. As soon as the paramedics came and I knew she was safe, I burst into tears—not from fear but from the release of guilt and a wave of relief. While I wouldn't wish the experience on anyone, finally being able to support my daughter through one of these moments because I had carved out time and space for my family meant I could begin to forgive myself. Elliott has new doctors and we're working together to formulate the best course of action for her, something I might have struggled to be as present for had I not changed my circumstances.

We've all heard the expression, "Don't get so busy on making a living that you forget to work on making a life." I used to roll my eyes and think, "Well, if you want to grow in your career, you have to work hard!" I now realize that there is far more to it. If you strive to do your best work every day and can do so as a well-rested person who feels respected and appreciated as an employee, you will still do great things. Balance and boundaries are necessary to prevent burnout and to ensure you are the best version of yourself for you, your family, and your place of work.

My advice to those who are burning the candle at both ends yet don't feel fulfilled and happy is to ask yourself "Why do I do it?" Dig down deep to find the motivation behind the behavior and start there. I gave myself space to really understand my "why" and realized that my fear of disappointing others and fear of failure created a perfect storm. It caused me to work (and worry) far too much in order to prove myself to my coworkers and to the organization at large. I rarely said no for fear of the assumption I was not capable of completing the task or rising to the challenge.

I've learned through this process that I have non-negotiables in my life. I will make it my priority to eat dinner with my family. I will not leave for work so early in the morning and arrive home so late that I do not see my children for days on end. For the rest of my career, I will ensure that my core values align with any company I choose to work for and represent. In big ways and small ways, I've made a promise to myself that I won't ever again get too busy making a living that I forget to work on making a life.

Throughout her career, Brooke Sieb has held positions in corporate accounting, wealth management client service, business analysis, operations, and technology. Her diverse background has provided her with a multi-faceted knowledge base and skill set in business process and technology, and invaluable experience in building relationships with clients and colleagues.

Brooke graduated from Quincy University in Quincy, Illinois, with a degree in Finance. She has also earned a certificate in Change Management from Washington University in St. Louis, Missouri.

Brooke is an active volunteer for Junior Achievement and fully supports their mission to promote financial capability, work and career readiness, and business ownership.

Outside of the office, Brooke enjoys a home life where she gets to pack school lunches and shuttle her children to their various practices. In her free time, she enjoys traveling with her family and sneaking away for dinner dates with her husband.

www.linkedin.com/in/brookesnidersieb/

Erika Nilles-Plumlee

Choosing Growth

I was in a place I had never been before, physically and mentally. My cheerful demeanor did not match the feelings I had inside. As I sat alone for the first months after losing my mom following her extended illness and my relocating to St. Louis, I was at a crossroads. Excited to be in a new city, alive with energy and promise, I was also unsettled and uncertain. I wanted to jump in and contribute somewhere but did not know how to start. With my career, which I'd chosen for a reason, I felt it was time to explore new possibilities, though I did not know what that meant or how to get there. Panic and self-doubt crept in, and my motivation disappeared.

Reflecting on other times in my life when I felt stuck or knew there was something I wanted to accomplish but did not know how to get started, themes of growth and resilience began to emerge. The first theme was seizing the moment or opportunity. When I wanted to do things like running a marathon, I signed up before I had ever run more than ten miles. By signing up, I would force myself to complete the training and the race. The second theme was perseverance. As a teen, I had a season-ending knee injury following two years of verbal and physical abuse from my coach. Through it all, I was determined to play sports. After moving with my family to a new town and promptly having knee surgery, I pushed myself through a year of rehabilitation and processed the mental abuse. This built my courage and confidence to play sports again. Another important theme was considering my "why." By staying true to myself and what was important to me—contributing to a world where everyone has opportunities for success—I would be able to step into the unknown and explore new opportunities.

As a young teen, I wanted to be a basketball player. To improve my game, I grabbed my basketball and rode my bike to neighborhoods where some of the best basketball players in the city played. After making the high school team, I noticed that several of the other very talented girls whom I played with regularly had to turn down their spot on the team. They could not commit to attending practice every day because they did not have reliable transportation or had responsibilities for caring for younger siblings after school. I was shocked, and humbled. Even though I worked hard to earn my starting position on the team, I knew deep down that there was an element of luck and good fortune to my success. The injustice in this situation was never lost on me and as I matured, and I knew I wanted to be part of the solution.

As I explored careers, I wanted to help others and work toward social justice. Without a mentor to help sort out what that looked like, choosing a career in social work seemed like a logical choice. I pursued a bachelor's degree in social work followed by a master's degree in social work administration. I worked in this field for several years in both the social service and criminal justice arenas. In some ways my path made complete sense, but I could not shake the feeling that there was something else I was supposed to be doing.

It's hard to walk away from something comfortable. After relocating to St. Louis, I first researched jobs based on my previous experience and became increasingly frustrated when nothing materialized. I felt completely disheartened and discouraged. Without recognizing it at the time, sitting in this discomfort was part of my path forward. I realized I was casting blame externally and instead started focusing on what was in my control. This experience became an opportunity—my shot at a career change.

I read books and listened to podcasts on personal development. I took strengths assessments and personal assessment inventories. Rather than trying to connect the assessment results to a specific career, I positioned them as my transferable skills. I also started sharing with colleagues and friends that I was interested in business, something that, years ago, I never considered because I mistakenly thought it may conflict with my values.

Through a networking opportunity, I connected with the owner of a St. Louis–based company. The original intent of the meeting was to gain insight and ideas about how to transition into the business world, yet I left the meeting with a part-time employment offer at her company. They needed help with specific projects, and there were also concerns with employee turnover and the work culture. I thought back to the time I naively signed up for my first marathon, trained hard, and ended up qualifying for the Boston Marathon. If I put myself into this uncomfortable situation, I knew I would figure out how to succeed. I knew nothing about the industry but trusted what I had uncovered during my recent personal assessment process. Confident my strengths were transferable, I accepted the position.

I immediately became a contributor by accomplishing any task I was assigned. A few months later, I was offered the Human Resources Manager position. I said "yes" before I even had the opportunity to realize how unprepared and underqualified I was. It was a reminder that saying "yes" to opportunities, rather than focusing on the reasons they would not work, was a crucial first step to my own growth. It meant ignoring all the negative thoughts that held me back and saying "yes" before overanalyzing.

Although confident in my people skills, I lacked business acumen, so I spent the next year learning everything I could about the human resources (HR) profession. I looked to professional organizations for training opportunities, became active (as a mentee) in a mentoring program, achieved my Society for Human Resource Management (SHRM) Certified Professional credentialing, and built my professional network. As my knowledge and confidence grew, I embraced roles that took me out of my comfort zone and viewed them as opportunities rather than challenges. My next stretch was moving from being a participant in these activities to being a leader by accepting a board position and becoming a presenter on topics relevant to my new career.

Reconnecting with my "why" was a crucial piece of my continued growth. A coach once told me I was a leader: people followed me, and I set the tone for our team. I did not understand the significance of this at the time, but now I began to understand the importance of this trait as a leader of people. This coach encouraged me and pointed out my strengths where the abusive coach from high school focused on weakness and relied on threats and intimidation. I came to see the significance of my professional role, and that I had not only the opportunity but the responsibility to develop others in becoming the best version of themselves personally and professionally. This benefitted the company as well, because when people are doing their best work, companies thrive.

Developing employees by providing opportunities, skill development, and recognition was something I had done throughout my career. Drawing on my previous education and experience, I applied the social work principle of starting where the client is and modified it to fit the business world. I began addressing employee needs the same way and designed a work environment where people were valued for their differences and strengths. Growth opportunities became part of the work culture. I looked for informal leaders, those who coworkers turned to and respected but did not hold formal leadership titles, and mentored them through an informal leadership program that integrated both professional and personal development. I exposed them to new and different opportunities, which had a big impact on my own growth too. Witnessing their success was a powerful motivator in my own continued development.

I recently accepted an executive-level HR position with a middle-market company with locations throughout the Midwest. This opportunity has challenged me yet again to think about growth strategically and systemically rather than individually. With greater reach and responsibilities, the time and attention I devote to growth-related activities has increased exponentially, both for me and those within my scope of influence.

Without recognizing it at the time, the choices and small steps I took to take control of my own growth after facing the tragic loss of my mom and relocating to a new community expanded and built on my strengths and previous life experiences. Everyone's path in life is different. Growth is personal and looks different for each person. Some days you're moving in leaps and bounds, and other days it's just putting one foot in front of another. However, for growth to occur, you must act. You may not have a clear vision of the destination but must be willing to say "yes" to opportunities that take you out of your comfort zone, while trusting and building on your strengths and following your "why" as the guiding principle.

Erika Nilles-Plumlee is a dynamic leader focused on aligning business strategy with people strategy. She is a strategic partner providing guidance on talent acquisition, positive employee engagement, and retention. She effectively collaborates with internal and external stakeholders to maintain organizational alignment and is an influencer across all levels of the company in support of operational and financial objectives.

Erika is currently the Director of Human Resources for StoneBridge Senior Living, a mid-market company headquartered in St. Charles with locations throughout the Midwest. Prior to StoneBridge Senior Living, Erika was the HR Manager for Lyons Blow Molding, a plastic bottle-manufacturing company where she improved company culture by creating a meaningful approach to employee growth and development. Erika also worked for the Kansas Department of Corrections developing and overseeing programs throughout the criminal justice system.

Erika enjoys spending time with her family and friends, exploring new restaurants, running, biking, hiking, playing pickleball, or working in her community garden.

www.linkedin.com/in/erikanillesplumlee/

b.Marcell Williams

Go – Fight – Winning

GO

One of my greatest joys and treasurers in life was giving birth to Jewels, Inc., a nonprofit youth mentoring organization I founded during my senior year at Howard University. Jewels honors the life and legacy of my grandmother and father who've passed away.

When my father passed away during my sophomore year in college, the grief nearly destroyed me. My father was a major source of confidence for me while I was growing up. He and my mother poured into me the belief that I could achieve anything. On October 19, 2004, my father, Peter Buckner, an executive at Annie Malone Children's Home, was snatched away from our family, friends, and loved ones while running an errand for the center. The young fourteen-year-old boy who smashed into the Annie Malone cargo van, which ejected my father from his seat, managed to hop out of the SUV he had stolen and run away from the scene.

When the accident happened, I was studying in the basement of Founder's Library at Howard University in Washington DC. The minimal cell phone signal there helped me focus on my work. After working hours upon hours to complete my tasks and assignments, I came up for air. The moment a friend of mine and I took a step out of the library, my phone dinged with notifications. We walked to the student center to grab dinner.

As I ordered my food, my mom called my cell phone. She asked me if I had any homework assignments or tests coming up. Having just spent hours in the library, I assured her I was good to go. She then told me that my father had been killed. I asked her, "Which one?" (I was raised by my stepfather since I was a two-year-old.) My knees buckled. My tray with my Chick-fil-A sandwich, fries, and lemonade barely made it onto the cashier's rack. My friend caught me and walked me over to a booth. My Howard University family comforted me that night. My mentor and her father drove me to the airport the next morning and sent me on my way with loads of love.

While on the airplane, I was so confused at how the world kept going. I felt as if my entire world had paused, stopped even. How could everyone keep showing up for work? Why were people driving their vehicles? What were they doing? My father had just been killed. The man who showed me what true unconditional love looked like was no longer on this earth. At home, I greeted a sea of blurred faces who loved the man just as much as I did. This was the moment that I unknowingly met depression face-to-face, and I would continue to deal with it for almost fifteen years. My father's death and my depression would play a huge role in my decision-making moving forward and my development as a young woman.

FIGHT

I returned to school in time for the famous Howard Homecoming festivities. I was a Bison Blue Squad (Varsity) Cheerleader and my father had planned to attend this homecoming experience prior to his death. He never made it. At the time of his death, I had a 3.6 GPA, was part of the top-tier organizations on campus, and a varsity cheerleader, all while working at BET and The Cheesecake Factory. I was making myself and my family proud. After my dad's death, I failed every single class, semester after semester. I would do well up until midterms, then flunk out. It was a trauma response to what I experienced with his death. "Therapy" in its finest form was not the therapy that I was introduced to back in the early 2000s. My understanding of therapy back then was that you go if something is "seriously" wrong and need to be placed in a psychiatric ward. So I didn't bother. I decided to self-medicate and wear a mask of service.

Running back and forth from on-campus responsibilities (class and organizational leadership) to off-campus responsibilities (work and family) kept me distracted. But in my travels, I started to have this unexplainable annoyance when I saw young girls hanging out after school and not involved in any extracurricular activities. I decided to do something about it and gift these beautiful black and brown girls with a role model. I created Jewels, Inc. to serve as an outlet for girls, ages 5–18+, to have a big sister and role model to help take them from one level to the next. Jewels, Inc. became my purpose, and these girls became my "jewels."

This program was an opportunity for me to pour positivity into the lives of the girls who came from the community that has given so much to me, Washington, DC. Jewels, Inc. became my battle cry. I would go on to pour my blood, sweat, and tears into this organization. I didn't finish at Howard "on time" because I gave all of myself to my Jewels. I fed them, gave them money to pay for classes when they were about to be dropped, and made sure they had everything they needed. I sacrificed so much to give all that I could give to pour into these young ladies the same level of confidence that my father poured into me. On campus, I fought for my Jewels. People didn't understand what I was doing, so they talked bad about us "just meeting." I stood in the gap for Jewels, Inc., and did everything I could until I couldn't.

WINNING

Things happen, people come and go, seasons change. During the pressure process of building Jewels, Inc., I was unknowingly draining myself. During this day and time, "self-care" was working yourself to the bone to be the best and do the best. There were zero markers for me to pause and take time to heal from the trauma I had experienced when I lost my father. There was a beautiful gift I was given out of all of this: the birth of my son. When I found out I was carrying life within my womb, I made the intentional decision to see this life come to light, and I nicknamed this seed PJ: "Pride and Joy" for a boy, "Precious Jewel" for a girl. My son's name is Peter James—my father's first name and his father's middle name. Naming him with the initials PJ was a complete coincidence. PJ was the best thing that could have ever happened *for me.* My son gave me the strength to begin growing out of my depression. I was given life just when the life that has forever changed me was taken away from me. My son literally woke me up to the fact that I should now focus on what I needed to get done for myself and for him.

I will forever love my Jewels; however, Peter's birth would become the starting point of my individual growth and healing. I had to step back, get to know myself while building a family, and allow Jewels, Inc. to grow organically from the foundation of blood, sweat, tears, and finances that I had poured into it like a tsunami. Jewels, Inc. thrived from this foundation. Jewels found her voice. Jewels grew and expanded. Jewels is now growing through another growth spurt, a rebirth—a redefining moment for our future. Taking the reins of Jewels, Inc. is no easy feat for any of our leaders; however, now is the time. Jewels, Inc. successfully completed JEWELTEENTH 2022: A Premier Juneteenth Celebration, the first-ever government-sponsored Juneteenth event to happen in the City of St. Louis, Missouri. Jewels has so much more to offer. We will continue to grow.

To *every* woman, no matter your age, background, etc., I encourage you to pursue your passions with a full heart. Life is so precious, and tomorrow is not guaranteed. The pressures behind creating, building, and growing Jewels, Inc. have always been on my mind. Since giving birth to Jewels, Inc., there has never been a moment when my Jewels were not on my mind, even with everything I have going on. I am now a wife and mother of five beautiful children. Do not let your circumstances or loss stop you from winning. Winning seasons are all around us; we must find the winning pieces and place them into one puzzle so we can see the bigger picture.

To learn more about my journey with Jewels, Inc., overcoming depression, and all the things, sign up for notifications of my book, *Go, Fight, Winning: A Guide to Overcoming Obstacles*, release date: October 24, 2022. www.bmarcell.com

b.Marcell Williams is a Communications & Business Strategist & Logistics Specialist by profession; Planning & Productivity Producer by passion; and author, speaker, women's & youth advocate by purpose. Mrs. Williams is the Senior Manager of Employer Brand and Talent Marketing at Anheuser-Busch, and owner of b.Marcell Enterprises, LLC, where she helps clients maximize resources, leverage their skill sets, and activate their dreams. Her most recent treasures were spearheading the groundbreaking 314 Day 2022 that united all St. Louis area communities for a five-day city-wide event, and producing Jewels, Inc.'s JEWELTEENTH: the first-ever government-sponsored Juneteenth event in the city of St. Louis.

She is the founder of Jewels, Inc. (a national 501(c)(3) focused on girls' mentoring & enrichment programs) and Brunch & Bible (a national women's ministry focused on helping women of all ages and backgrounds create and/or enhance their relationship with Jesus). A proud Howard University alum, b.Marcell is a wife and mother of five beautiful children.

www.bmarcell.com/
www.jewelteenth.com/
www.instagram.com/bmarcellwins/
www.instagram.com/jewelsinc
www.instagram.com/jewelteenth
www.linkedin.com/in/bmarcellwilliams

Shannon Norman

Goodbye Ramen Noodles

One unexpected phone call was the beginning of a life-changing journey. This journey is comparable to a plant growing from a tiny little seed. You see, I found myself living on my own, independently, at the age of eighteen. As a young child, I had only a few memories of everything we owned being auctioned off, with no idea what bankruptcy meant. As far as I could tell, it meant that a bunch of farm equipment was taken. Even worse, food we used to buy at the grocery store was replaced with whatever wild game (rabbit and squirrels and deer) was available. Yuck!

A college education wasn't a priority in my family. At age sixteen, I knew very little about college, and I began working any time I wasn't in school. The goal was to be able to support myself to escape the abusive home life I had grown up in. In high school, I completed a vocational program in business at the local community college. I knew just enough to know that I needed more education beyond high school. So I worked multiple jobs at the same time I earned my associate's degree. My thought was that a two-year degree would be all I needed to reach financial stability.

A family member convinced me the best next step was to find a job with the State of Missouri, which would give me stability and benefits. I completed the lengthy application process, including multiple tests, and soon found myself working in human resources. Early on, I felt so accomplished making $17,000 a year with amazing benefits, paid by the state. I met incredible people and learned quickly, leading to a promotion, but I still wasn't making much money.

At the time, I was living with a few friends in a very old farmhouse that was infested with cockroaches and had urine and feces stains in the carpet from the previous tenant. Part of the agreement with the landlord was we would get a "good" rental rate if we cleaned up the house and did some improvements. I recall the fear I had when considering another path… the idea of no longer being a tenant but rather purchasing a mobile home (trailer house). While I wanted a nicer place to live, the thought of buying a trailer for $16,500 scared the you-know-what out of me. Yep, $16,500 caused me many agonizing sleepless nights worrying about making the payments as well as other associated expenses. (Who knew that years later I would spend the same amount on a deck to my new home!)

I wanted something nice so badly, I could taste it! The trailer had been a lake home and was like new. It had an air conditioner and a heating system with a thermostat on the wall and a garbage disposal and beautiful cabinets. I had never lived in a house with all these comforts. I grew up in a hundred-year-old house with no foundation. That house was infested with whatever rodents found their way inside, especially mice and rats! In junior high school, I spent $65 of my own money on a pair of popular British Knight high-top shoes that ended up with a nest of dead mice inside. If that wasn't bad enough, a friend of mine was visiting when I discovered the nest. I was mortified! I had to throw away my prized high tops because I could not get rid of the horrific stench. To this day, the smell of these dead creatures makes me want to vomit! Enough with these memories of darkness; I'll stick with my desire to do more with my life.

I purchased the trailer house and enjoyed it for a few years. Then along came some other life-changing events (having nothing to do with finances) that resulted in me living in a bad part of town in a small, but cheap, duplex. At this stage in life, I was racking up credit card debt and living on Ramen noodles. I frequently thought, "Please, no more Ramen noodles!" The one thing I was certain of was that this was *not* the life I wanted to live. Like the journey of a growing plant, I was starving for water and sunlight.

And then the phone call. A potential life-changing path. My dear mother called to say she was going to college! This is the amazing woman who started a family very young and did her best to keep me and my siblings safe during a more than twenty-year abusive relationship with my father. Her priority was taking care of three small children. She hadn't had the time, resources, or support to continue her education. But now she was at the stage in her career that if she wanted to be more than a secretary, she needed a degree. She told me about a program that would allow her to keep her day job and go to school locally at night. Would I be interested in doing the same program? I quickly shut her down, explaining that I didn't have the money. She said she was having a packet of information mailed to me anyway for further consideration. I now see that this invitation was the water and sunlight I hungered for.

When the packet arrived in the mail, I began dreaming about what my life could look like if I had a bachelor's degree. But how could I ever make this work? That's when the next important call came, from my mother again. This time she invited me to move into her basement, rent free! This got my attention. She described how we could be in the same cohort but different groups; she had already confirmed the details with the adviser.

Fast-forward: Together we graduated with our bachelor's degrees (William Shatner gave the commencement speech), and we enjoyed the quality time living under one roof. This was an entirely different experience than when I was a child. By this time, she was divorced and living in a brand-new home in a very nice subdivision. We made up for lost time, and it was one of the best chapters in my life. The tiny seed was breaking through the soil.

Not long after obtaining my degree, I received a big promotion that I wouldn't have been considered for without my education level. And soon after, another promotion. Now I was making a whopping $40,000 a year! I was so proud and had a huge sense of accomplishment. It wasn't long before I was eager to take the next leap and get my MBA. I was a little uncomfortable being the oldest student in class, who worked full time and had a family. But I focused on my goal of continued growth and had faith that there was something even better ahead.

Growth is challenging for most people and doesn't come without discomfort and pain. I frequently think of how a tiny seed is planted in soil where it is dark and lonely. When I get in a rut in life, this is how I feel: lonely, out of sight, and in the dark. When the time is right, after some sunlight and water, the seed grows into something beautiful. Its development is a process. Its beauty cannot be rushed. Like our lives, when we grow, development is a process. We may be capable of speeding up the process through planning and diligence, but as with the tiny seed, our development takes time. We must focus on steps to move us in the direction we want to go, rather than focusing on it not happening fast enough or seeing ourselves as a victim of a bad situation. The sunlight and water, for us, are our mindset, actions, and support system. We must figure out how to consistently be in a productive mindset, be accountable, and surround ourselves with people who believe in us. This is my hope for you!

My story started with a phone call from my mother, followed by decisions and hard work. I chose my paths to success with numerous challenges throughout my journey. I shed many tears and questioned my abilities along the way. I'm grateful I had a strong support system and the determination and diligence to dig out of a place of poverty. My message to anyone reading this is that you have more control than you may think. You *can* reach those goals that feel like a dream. Start with one small step at a time, and the goal feels more realistic. As we take steps forward, sometimes we get pushed back, but that's when we must talk kindly to ourselves and consult with the people who believe in us! "A journey of a thousand miles begins with a single step," the famous Chinese proverb reminds us. Take your first step now and be confident you will succeed!

Shannon Norman is an *Inclusion of Women in Leadership* coach, speaker, human resources executive leader, and the founder of the movement Accept The Compliment™. Shannon helps women in male-dominated industries break through the glass ceiling. Using her methods, her clients have the tools to get the promotion they deserve.

Shannon has over twenty years of experience in Human Resources, coaching hundreds along the way. In addition to holding a Senior Certified Professional Certificate in Human Resources, she is also certified by the International Coaching Federation, the gold standard in the coaching industry.

Shannon holds an MBA from Southeast Missouri State University Harrison College of Business. She was a nontraditional student who furthered her education as a working adult.

shannonnormancoaching@gmail.com
www.shannonnormancoaching.com
www.linkedin.com/in/shannonnorman/
www.facebook.com/shannonnormancoaching
www.instagram.com/norman.shannon/
www.tiktok.com/@shannonnormancoaching
573-239-3443

Michelle Steeg

Just Jump

Educational institutions were never going to be ready for me, and I didn't know. I just didn't know...

My entire career, I have been surrounded by men. My two mentors were men, I specialize in treating men, and at the end of my career in education, I was working in an all-boys high school with over six hundred male students and a predominantly all-male faculty. My experience with men was the catalyst and Achilles' heel to my story of growth.

After graduating with my master's in Professional Counseling, I immediately opened my practice. I ran an intensive outpatient treatment program (IOP) for adolescent males who had tested positive for drugs. I absolutely loved working with these young men. They were tough, no bullshit, and they respected me, as did I them. At one point I remember thinking, "What if I could get to them and reach them before they got to me?" This question started my journey into education. I never really wanted to be in education but decided to become certified in school counseling. What I wanted was access to kids so I could teach mental health on a bigger scale. I've worked in six different buildings crossing the K–12 spectrum, but high schoolers were where it was at for me.

Looking back over the schools I served in the last decade, I now see that my role was to be the domino—the domino that provokes, initiates, and insists on change. In my case, the change surrounded teaching mental health in our schools. Every school I entered was truly excited to have me there because I was never afraid to rock the boat for the benefit of its students. This is also precisely what confused me about how I felt leaving every situation. Educators and administrators say they want change surrounding mental health and yet are terrified of it. Making changes in education is like driving a car with the parking brake on. I was the catalyst for change they said they wanted, but each time the dominos began to fall, the cascade would come to a screeching halt.

There were a lot of things that happened during my tenure in education that led to my decision to leave. Surprisingly, the #MeToo Movement forced me to be the domino in my own life. It was an awakening. Words cannot adequately express what happened to me emotionally and physically during that time. After all the years of trying to get the men I worked with to take me seriously, trying to prove my value, the years of being spoken over, the years of forcing myself to hold back tears of fear and anger, the #MeToo Movement saw me and validated me. I felt righteous anger. I felt completely seen. As story after story unfolded, and as I watched man after man exposed as the abuser he was, I became emboldened in my pursuit of growth and success. It was always there before, but something profound shifted inside me.

Then the moment happened—the moment I needed to jump. For the first time in my thirteen years of practicing part time, my anger finally overrode any fear I had of not being able to sustain a private practice full time. And just like that, there was no turning back. I decided right then and there that I would never work for a man (or anyone else) again. I kept the decision private for about two weeks while I worked out the logistics. Then, one evening in the early winter of 2017, I told my husband my decision. I said I was done with education and wanted to invest in myself and practice full time. He didn't bat an eye. He was on board for the jump and told me he believed in me and didn't have a doubt I would be successful. A week later, I asked my office mate (and former mentor) to let me take over the lease of the office we shared. He also didn't hesitate. Making this jump—investing in myself—allowed the most important people in my life, who happened to be men, to invest right back. This was the nutrient-rich soil I needed to continue to grow in my decision.

As I sat with this decision to jump to the next level, I made another decision. I vowed that in 2018 I was going to do everything that scared the shit out of me. We cannot grow and stay in the safety of our comfort zone. Pushing through fear and insecurity promises growth. So, I began compiling a list of things I wanted to do that I couldn't do while being tied to a desk in education. I also promised myself that if I was really going to leave education, I was going to do it my way. I was going to be unapologetically myself, even if it meant turning people off, losing potential clients, or leaving money on the table. My growth meant stepping fully into who I am as a human being, woman, and entrepreneur. I was going to make this change as the most authentic version of myself possible. I can say with confidence that I have accomplished this goal. This authenticity is what draws people to me . . . to any of us. I believe women have been taught to edit and censor themselves because society and patriarchy have taught us what women should be, sound like, and act like. Fuck that. If you want growth, throw away the fucking rule book. Tap into your intuition that has been silenced for a lifetime and listen to your own voice, not society's.

Due to the #MeToo Movement and several disappointing experiences, I left my career in education feeling very much like a woman scorned. I was hell-bent that if I was going to build this practice, I was going to do it by only supporting other female business owners. So I hired a female web designer, accountant etc. I decided I was going to build my practice by working with only women. I was going to take my energy and expertise and support other women in fulfilling their dreams. Before my first year of full-time private practice was over, I felt like something was missing. I was in a counseling session with my therapist, discussing my work with boys and men. She observed that my face absolutely lights up when I talk about them. She's not wrong. It's where my professional love lies. In fact, my favorite clients to work with are men who think therapy is bullshit. But wait! I'm supposed to be out here championing for and supporting women to reach their greatest personal and professional goals. And yet something was missing.

On a podcast interview for female entrepreneurs, I volunteered to let the host pick my brain on a challenge I was experiencing in my business. Here's what came out of the discussion: I needed permission to follow my desire to work with a population that sets my soul on fire. I got so caught up in #MeToo and my own experiences with a professional lifetime of feeling disregarded by men that I felt I would be betraying women if I chose to work with men. The interview spurred another moment of growth during the year that I vowed to do everything that scared the shit out of me. I discovered the most profound and beautiful truth: if my goal is to truly help women, the greatest way I can accomplish this is to help heal their men, to educate and give them emotionally intelligent, safe, strong, and secure men. To date, I have worked with more women (simply because more women seek counseling) in my career as an LPC, but I specialize in working with men, and intend to grow my practice with them.

Growth comes in all shapes and sizes. Growth is not linear. Growth is scary. Feeling scared should be the first inclination that you are on the right track. If you're looking for growth, start small. My goal of doing everything that scared me wasn't all huge things. It was mostly small steps out of my comfort zone with a few giant ones sprinkled in.

Just jump. If you are considering leaving a job, please hear me say this: That moment you are waiting for, that perfect moment that gives you the validation to leave, is never coming. Because the truth is, it's already come and gone many times over, and you chose to ignore it. What I can promise you will come is the validation that you made the right choice by investing in yourself and leaving. I had to surrender to the truth. Education was never going to be ready for me, and that's OK. I loved my time in education because it brought me to where I am today. My students fed my soul and taught me more than they could ever begin to imagine. Once I surrendered to this truth, there was nothing left to do but jump. It turned out to be the greatest decision I have ever made.

Michelle Steeg is a licensed professional counselor (LPC) in practice for fifteen years. Michelle received her master's degree in Professional Counseling from Webster University in 2008. Soon after opening her practice, she received her certification in K–12 School Counseling from Lindenwood University. Michelle spent ten years serving in administrative roles advocating for mental health education in schools. In 2018 Michelle left her tenure in education to pursue her dream of practicing full time and has never looked back.

Michelle has an unconventional approach to the traditional world of therapy. She is a mental health advocate who loves speaking to organizations about women in leadership and providing professional development that changes how the world sees and treats emotional health.

Michelle is a wife and mother to a mischievous and loving boy. She is personally touched by and speaks up for Parkinson's research and dyslexia advocacy. Michelle's soul lies in traveling, scuba diving, dogs, and cooking.

www.michellesteeg.com
www.facebook.com/michelle.russosteeg
www.instagram.com/msteeg22/
www.twitter.com/Msteeg22

Katie Wilson

Stories of Mentors and Growth

Let Me Help You

Transitioning from student to professional is not always the easiest step, but if you are fortunate enough to have wonderful mentors along the way, the journey can be filled with growth. When you are just starting out, you want to be competent and fulfill your duties and responsibilities, but at some point you are going to make mistakes or not know what to do. You do not know everything, it is impossible to know everything, and the more open you are with everyone that you are not able to know and solve everything, the better. You need other folks to collaborate, brainstorm, and be part of your team. You need the right people on your bus in the right seats. You cannot be perfect, and the sooner you let yourself off this hook, the better. You also cannot get everything completed in a timely manner by yourself. You need others to be in alliance with you along this journey. Instead of trying to figure it out on your own, lean on mentors to assist you through the process.

When I began my journey as a teacher, I was given a mentor who helped shape me into an innovative educator who focused on trying and growing rather than being "right." I had other mentors who helped me understand that being an educator was more than content: It was about listening, learning, and building relationships with students. It was about being a role model and a mentor for the students. It was about compassion and empathy.

Here's a funny story: When I first began my education career, I was given a perceiver test, and I failed empathy. Now, I believe empathy is one of my greatest qualities and gifts that I can share with others.

I have transformed over my years in education from a person who wanted to listen, judge, and determine a "fix," to a person who listens deeply, is nonjudgmental about the situation, and doesn't offer advice unless solicited by the individual. It is important for students, especially young women, to have that person in their life who they can turn to and not be judged. You never know what someone is going through, but you can bet that they are going through something. Some students wear their needs on their faces, and they will share with you. Others are not so forthcoming, but it is necessary to offer them the same grace and patience even though you may not know their story. Sometimes they may not want to share or may not be able to share. Do not push them; instead, be the welcoming face, the warm smile, and the comforting space to spend some time with. I believe this is the best gift that I share with my students.

A Gentle and Safe Place

When interacting with other people, you do not know what is going on behind the scenes. I had a mentor tell me this as I transitioned from teacher to administrator. She told me that, more often than not, we need to stop talking, stop asking questions, and listen with our ears and heart—and remember that school should be a gentle and safe place for students to land. She shared the following story to illuminate this lesson, and it has stuck with me each and every day. Early on in her administrative career, a female student kept coming late to school. Finally, the administrator had enough of the student's tardiness and seeming carelessness about being on time for school. She confronted the student about this pattern and the consequences for her behavior. The student broke down and told the administrator that there were certain mornings that her mom must leave early for work, and that her stepfather abused her on those mornings and then dropped her off late to school. After a long conversation with the student about what could be done, the administrator reflected and resolved herself to never ask students why they were late to school or to other events. Instead, she would say, "I am really glad that you are here. I hope everything is going OK for you today."

This is a simple shift in mindset and communication, but what a change in how the other person feels! Instead of instantly putting them on the defensive, welcome them into the space and let them know how glad you are to see them and spend time with them. It takes effort and practice, but try to put yourself in the other person's shoes. As some may say, try to see it from their perspective or through their lens. Folks may not always remember what you talk about, but they will always remember how you made them feel. Be a gentle and safe place for folks.

Board of Directors

I was only able to work with this mentor for one year, but we have kept in touch because he had such an impact on me. I asked him to present at the last faculty meeting we had together, and he shared the Board of Directors concept. He asked the group to think of the five to seven people we would have on the "Board of Directors for Our Lives," both personally and professionally. He asked us to write their names down, the position they'd hold on our board, and why we chose to elevate them to our board. Once we had this information together, we shared in small groups, and then he asked us to contact each person on our board and let them know how important they are to our personal and professional lives. Connections – Communication – Dynamic Relationships – Gratitude. Sometimes we forget to thank those who have coached us, who have done so much for us along the way and who continue to help us grow.

Communication and Honest Feedback

Over the years, I have learned many challenges stem from miscommunication or the complete lack of communication. Email or text allows for a quick response, but often, a phone conversation or face-to-face (even if it is virtual) allows for better communication and connections, which lead to better relationship building. The closer we can grow in relationship, the more courageous conversations we can have with one another. In these brave spaces, we can offer and accept honest feedback to one another and ultimately grow.

A few years back I had a courageous conversation with a mentor, and we definitely did not see eye-to-eye on the situation. However, after multiple lengthy face-to-face conversations, I not only learned that I was wrong in this situation but that I needed to continue to learn and expand my knowledge in this area. I agreed to read articles, listen to podcasts, and watch videos, after which we would discuss my new knowledge. I had a multitude of questions along the way. I was fortunate that this individual was very open to my questions and to discussion on sensitive topics, and that he challenged me to continue to learn and grow.

I have been blessed to have been surrounded by amazing mentors throughout my education journey. These men and women gently reshaped my mindset toward education and, more broadly, life in general. It is my hope that these stories not only resonate with you but also help you to reflect on the mentors you have had through your career and the lessons they illuminated for you. Use the following section to guide you through the reflection process and work through the action items.

Reflection and Actions Items

1. Attitude of Gratitude. Recall the best mentors you have had in your personal and/or professional lives. Contact them and say thank you. Let them know how much of an impact they have had on your life.

2. Reflect on and write down the five to seven people on your Board of Directors. Then contact everyone to share that they hold a seat on your board and why you placed them there.

3. Reflect on your day and journal.

4. To continue building your growth mindset, determine some topics/concepts that you want to learn more about and then dig in.

Katie Wilson is currently embarking on an adventure. She is transitioning to a different career in a new city. She has over a decade of experience in single-sex secondary education as a teacher, coach, mentor, assistant principal, and principal. Katie earned a BS in Biology, an MS in Biology, her teacher certification, and an Educational Specialist Degree in Educational Leadership. She is a member of the Professional Women's Alliance of St. Louis and the Missouri Association of Secondary School Principals. Katie is passionate about mentoring and empowering young women to embrace fully who they are, to challenge themselves to be brave in their life journey, and to instill the courage to grow academically, socially, and emotionally. There is always room for growth.

katherine.vandeven@gmail.com

Shawna Daras

Grow With Me

When the alarm wakes me in the morning at this time in my life, I'm grateful for the day. It wasn't always this way.

Alarm (Beep, Beep, Beep)…No, I don't want to get up yet, I want to sleep.

I grew up in a small town of 17,000 in Indiana, an only child in a lower-middle class family. My parents were married throughout my childhood and divorced when I was an adult. I really don't recall many times that I saw them happy together. We moved around a lot and I attended three different elementary schools, one of those twice. With all the moving, I learned to be adaptable at a young age. My father has his GED, and my mother a high school diploma, so college wasn't discussed much and didn't seem to be important. After graduation, I decided I was not going to college. Then, my closest friends left for college and I quickly realized I wanted to go too. My mom registered me for community college classes.

During my high school days, I met a boy and "fell in love," and in 1992 at the age of nineteen, I married. Marriage came with more responsibilities, like bills. I quit the college classes and worked full time. My husband and I realized we wanted more, so we decided to go to nursing school together. I completed LPN school at Ivy Tech State College when I was twenty-one years old. From teenager to wife to nurse in three years was more growth than I wanted so quickly.

Divorced at the age of twenty-two, searching for my purpose, I decided to leave the small town I had known all my life and move to Indianapolis. I was working, making money, having fun, and sharing an apartment with my childhood first best friend, my cousin Debi (we were only ten months apart), and her four-year-old daughter. I was living my best life! Working with the pediatric population in home healthcare, I learned a lot about children with disabilities, their families, their struggles, and their wins. It was very humbling. I grew in empathy, patience, understanding. I welcomed this growth, and it taught me lessons I needed for future events in my life.

Again, I met a boy and fell in love. This newfound love brought me to St. Louis in 1998. I was twenty-six years old and dreaming of a family. We married in 2001 and immediately began infertility treatment. For four years followed the infertility protocol. On my thirtieth birthday, I cried on the steps of my home. Devastated that I couldn't have a baby, I was angry at God. "What is so bad about me that God doesn't want me to be a mom?" I wondered. A second round of IVF failed. We couldn't afford to try it again, so I came to the realization I was not going to experience pregnancy. I had two amazing stepsons whom I loved, but they had a mom. I wanted a child to call me "mom." I wanted the first day of kindergarten, I wanted to be the one they came to, to kiss their boo-boos. Adoption was my answer, or so I thought. My husband's and my combined ages were getting close to the requirement limit for domestic adoption, so we decided to adopt internationally. However, I paused the process, feeling I needed to take a year to think, contemplate, and let my hormones get back to normal from all the infertility treatments.

During that year, I received an explanation of benefits from my health insurance, which stated we had money left in our infertility coverage. I had one more shot at IVF: round three. Nine months later at the age

181

of thirty-four, I gave birth to the most beautiful baby boy. I apologized profusely to God! I learned life happens on his timeline, not mine. Thirty-three months later at the age of thirty-seven, along came my extra gift from God, a daughter. God knew just what I needed when he gifted me my daughter. She has taught her type A mom to embrace the spilled milk instead of crying over it. I think back to that day sitting and crying at the age of 30 crying on my steps, 7 years later I have a son and a daughter that just overflows my heart. Spiritual growth beyond what I could ever try to explain.

In 2018, the dream I chased my whole life was crumbling. My family, who I wanted more than anything, was ending, and I divorced. Kirkwood, Missouri, was all my children knew, and they pleaded, "Mom, please let us stay in our schools with our friends." Due to unforeseen circumstances, my salary would be the only source of income. Thinking about financial, emotional, and future needs was overwhelming when trying to decide what to do, or where to go. My children's plea to stay in Kirkwood gave me my mission. It wasn't easy, but it was worth it.

I purchased a townhouse close to their schools. We learned needs verses wants, and we had amazing support from church (who helped my kids attend camps), friends who surprised us with groceries and helped when needed with the kids, and so much more. My heart was so full of gratitude during yet another time of growth—growth in being humble and finding strength and determination.

A little over a year after my divorce and moving to the townhouse, my mom was visiting and woke me at four a.m. with terrible news: My cousin Debi, my childhood best friend and former roommate, had shot herself. After being taken off life support, four hours later she gained her angel wings. She was only forty-seven years old. After returning from her funeral in Indiana, the Suicide Walk was held in St. Louis. My twelve-year-old son said, "Mom, we are walking in the Suicide Walk for Aunt Debi." We got involved and learned how prevalent suicide is. Before Debi's death, part of me thought suicide was selfish, or a sin, or something other than what it is. Suicide is a tragic outcome of something much deeper. Without a doubt, there is no way Debi would have taken her own life if there wasn't something deeper going on. My cousin was the least selfish human I knew, and she loved God fiercely. I try to remember all the good times and smile, but I'm not quite OK with this loss yet, and the tears still flow. The discussions and questions with my kids about "Aunt Debi" were hard, but I have a whole new perspective on suicide. I grew.

At forty-six years of age, I was nowhere I thought I would be nor wanted to be. While being a mom is the most amazing thing in my life, being a mom is far from easy. Being a single mom without family near, and living in what I consider a more expensive community, was challenging, but I was determined to make it work. It was on me to make the life I could for my kids.

I am an LPN by trade, a Licensed Practical Nurse. After six years at my company, a BA IV (Business Analyst IV) position became available. Web portal work was out of my wheelhouse, a different kind of work than nursing. I was nervous about applying, but then I thought, "Why not?" I got the position! I took classes at University of Missouri–St. Louis and learned so much. I was totally out of my comfort zone but determined because this position would also provide additional financial support. With the new job, I sent my kids to camp without assistance from the church. For the next two years, I gained knowledge that would propel me forward to my current position as a project manager. My career went a whole new direction, and I grew!

As I turn fifty this year, I reflect on how I have grown throughout so many events in my life—more than can be written in this chapter. My story isn't any different than most other women's stories. My message to every person is: No matter what events, good or not so good, through your journey, keep it moving! Take time to laugh, to cry, to grieve, to share joy, to count your blessings, to propel forward and upward, to learn, to breath, to exhale, and to count on others. All the events in our lives make us grow. I am right where I am supposed to be, I now know. That doesn't mean there aren't times I yearn for things in my life, but I've learned to trust even when I can't see what's ahead.

Now, when I hear:

Alarm (Beep, Beep, Beep)…I open my eyes and say, "Good morning, God! Thank you for today, for opening my eyes, for my children, for all my blessings."

…and every day, I will continue to *grow*.

Shawna Daras is a Project Manager at Centene Corporation working in the Digital Solutions and Clinical Systems arena. Shawna is a Licensed Practical Nurse and began her career working with geriatric patients, then moved into caring for the pediatric population. When Shawna joined Centene, she worked in quality control, doing clinical auditing for Centene Health Plans. Over the last three years, Shawna has expanded on her career goals and branched out to the digital solutions world in her company and is looking forward to the future.

Outside of work, Shawna is doing what she absolutely loves the most in life, being a mom to her two amazing kiddos. Jake plays guitar and is on his way to completing his Eagle Scout. Autumn keeps mom busy with basketball, pageants, and anything else she can talk Mom into letting her do. Shawna and her kids spend a lot of time doing volunteer work.

s.daras@yahoo.com
www.linkedin.com/in/shawna-daras

Emily A. Thorne

What Ladder!?

"Rise and Grind."

"Grow through what you go through."

"Fake it until you make it."

When it comes to overused cliches about growth, the list goes on and on. There is a motivational quote or meme for every situation and/ or phase in life, both professional and personal. But the one that has always been a real head-scratcher for me has been *"Climbing the corporate ladder."* I clearly understand the meaning behind it, but it implies there is a one-size-fits-all type of career path out there for everyone, which is simply not true. I'd venture to say that for most contributors to this book, it's quite the opposite, as we've all carved out our own personal growth journey every step of the way. The happiest and most driven people I know did not use the "cookie cutter" approach to life. No sir. No easy button here. But that's the beauty in following what really drives you to succeed. I've spent my last twelve (short) years figuring out what gets my heart fired up and chasing that feeling down every chance I get. Seeing how far I've come by pushing myself outside of my comfort zone, I smile and ask, "What ladder!?"

Looking back on my path, I've realized I built my own ladder with every experience along the way, both good and not-so-good.

The first rung of my ladder is, without a doubt, *family.*

By the time I was twelve, I'd seen all parts of the country, from the beaches to the mountains. Around that time, our "travel family" went on a cruise together that changed my worldview. I'd been on several vacations like this, and it was common to see the over-the-top entertainment and endless buffets. One thing I wasn't familiar with was the harsh reality of a third-world country I was about to encounter between the port and tourist beach in Roatán, Honduras. We stepped off the cruise ship and had a crew staff taking professional pictures of our group while we were all laughing and smiling, carefree. We all loaded up into our chariot of the day, the Chevy Suburban, and started our voyage to our excursion for the day. When we drove away from the ship, we went through a ten-foot-tall chain-linked fence with barbed wire around the top. And if that wasn't prison-like enough, there were guards on both sides with semi-automatic weapons. No one batted an eye, just went along with their conversations. Did no one see this?

When we returned to the Roatán port, the moment I looked past those gates, I immediately broke into tears and had no appetite. I asked my dad, "How can we be so greedy? We have enough food to feed everyone on this island and here we are eating our third or fourth meal today." This was the first time I felt the passion of my *cultural empathy*, and I had no idea what it meant or what to do with that feeling. I had no idea it was going to be the drive behind my career and leadership style.

Necessity. At St. Pius X High School, I was the quiet, timid girl who enjoyed reading books and creating artwork…who fell in love with soccer. I was looking at a scholarship to SIUE my senior year until getting the tell-tale story of a small-town life, a positive pregnancy test just weeks before my high school graduation. I became a mother right after I turned nineteen. My parents helped me tremendously, but I told myself I refused to be another teen mom statistic.

Around the time my son was nine to ten months old, my mother started her own construction company, Midwest Construction Services and Products, mainly subcontracting to prime contractors on Department of Transportation projects throughout Missouri. Her projects paid prevailing wages, so I became a laborer on heavy highway jobsites to provide for myself and my son. Within the first year, I had jumped into the back-office side as well and figured out all the paperwork processes. By this time, I'd fallen in love with the construction industry and began to envision how I could combine it with the Legal Studies program at St. Louis Community College, where I was enrolled.

Willpower. Those were some of the hardest, most physically taxing summers of my life working with the Midwest employees who would become like family. They knew I cared about them and getting the job done well. They saw me reading the blueprints and contracts, familiarizing myself with project details. They were my allies in a male-dominated landscape. I remember countless times we would be on-site and the inspectors and/or the project manager would walk directly past me or not even look in my direction when asking about our work. My crew would straighten them out, quickly telling them I was their point of contact.

Community. Years later, I knew that to grow I needed to branch away from Midwest. My first glimpse into the corporate construction world was my preconstruction role at Clayco, where I met some of the most amazing people and I was introduced to NAWIC (National Association of Women in Construction). The leadership, networking, and confidence this group brought me is unprecedented. With NAWIC members, I felt seen and understood for the first time. The leadership opportunities there gave me the confidence in myself to keep growing and being the best version of myself.

Mentorship. My next role was with Tarlton. Within my first few months, a shift in leadership brought me a new supervisor, COO Dirk Elsperman. Dirk was National Association of General Contractors (AGC) President and was extremely busy traveling with this position, but he never stopped his one-on-one contact and check-ins with his direct reports at Tarlton. He was a real leader, always encouraging me to step outside my comfort zone. Public speaking was an obstacle to me, and he told me a handful of times, "This is a friendly group. They're here to hear what you have to say."

Failure. After three years with Tarlton, I was looking for upward growth when a high-pressure recruiter jumped into the picture and promised the world. I believed them. The company culture in my new role, however, was not a good fit. I struggled mentally and felt a sense of guilt for "jumping ship," but I had to do what was right for me. I resigned from the new position after four short months. I learned a lesson that will stick with me the rest of my life: if you are not happy, you have every right to make a change regardless of the situation. This change came in the form of my current role at ADB Companies as Contracts Manager, a role that feels like it was made for me.

Appreciation. In Chapter 4 of *Emotional Intelligence for the Modern Leader,* a book my colleagues and I chose to read together, Christopher D. Connors writes:

> *Your direction determines the actions you must take to*
> *fulfill the requirements of your why. Too often, new leaders*
> *doubt themselves because they don't think they're READY to*
> *begin moving in the direction of what they want to accom-*
> *plish. They think it's not their time, that they're lacking in*

a particular area, or that they're simply too young. They're hindered by limiting beliefs that beget doubt and fear.

Growth. It is uplifting when an experience in life "comes full circle" or you "reap what you sow." When I was first asked to contribute to this book, I hesitated for several reasons.

"Me? Emily Thorne? Are you sure you have the right person?"

During our introduction call with the other contributors, we shared a little about ourselves and how we help people. After hearing these amazing women introduce themselves, I was terrified, and was certain I couldn't stand alongside them. As reluctant as I was, I put together a general outline of my story. One thing led to another, and I remembered parts of my journey that I had forgotten. My story was telling itself. My voice. My story. The ups, the downs, the highs, the lows, and everything in between. That self-doubt vanished.

My advice to you: Stop the self-doubt. What you have to offer the world is more than enough. Find what gets your blood pumping, *start building your own ladder*, and never look back. If my story can help just one person out there find their true passion and voice, then I've succeeded. My story is worth being heard. And so is yours.

Reflection. The universe has blessed me beyond measure with the people I've met, the experiences I've had, and the mindset I've been given. I wouldn't be who I am today without those interactions that each taught me a lesson, both good and bad. And this is only the beginning. Here's my last saying, "There's no such thing as loses, only wins and lessons."

Emily A. Thorne is the Contracts Manager at ADB Companies with over ten years of construction experience in various firms across the St. Louis region, focused on process improvement and legal operations. She began her construction career as a laborer on DOT projects before starting in contract management. She earned her AAS for Legal Studies from St. Louis Community College and holds a Construction Industry Technician certification through the American Council for Construction Education.

Emily serves as Immediate Past President on the board of directors for the local St. Louis Chapter of NAWIC (#38)—National Association of Women in Construction. She was named Midwest Region's Future Leader of the Year in 2021 by NAWIC. She's involved in diversity and education efforts at student outreach events and career days, bringing awareness to career opportunities in the construction industry. She currently serves on ADBTogether Committee, ADB's cultural pillar to encourage and promote diversity, equity, and inclusion.

www.linkedin.com/in/emilythorne1

Jeanie Brewster

A Gentle Soul Reminder

Wow. This chapter might be out of left field from the other growth chapters you are reading, but I followed my inner thoughts when I started to write, and this is the result. This chapter took a turn even I didn't expect. I hope you enjoy!

"A gentle soul." Those are the words people used to describe my mother (Kathleen) at eighty-nine years young. As friends and relatives reflected at Mother's memorial services this past year, the words had a new meaning to me. A *gentle soul*. Hmmm. These words fit my mother because of her love and kindness to all whom her life touched, but also a shockwave hit me (that is, hit me over the head and felt like a big goose egg kind of knot on a bald man's head). The shockwave had two parts: I would become a grandmother this year, and the words "gentle soul" are not said in association with my name. I wondered: "Is the legacy of a gentle soul leaving the family with my generation?"

I'm "Jeanie B" in business, and no one wanted to ask where the "B" came from. That was fine with me, working in the man's world of business. Let others think what they wanted. It didn't bother me; it gave me space to do my work and succeed where others had not. Those who did know me knew it stood for my last name…ha ha! It is not uncommon for women in the business world to leave out the last name for privacy and safety reasons, so I just let those others believe whatever. Why spend time correcting those who didn't appreciate/respect a woman's knowledge to lead and own her own company, anyway? I was on a career path of forward with the throttle pushed all the way down, hitting the curves on two wheels.

A gentle soul. Are you kiddin' me? Is that supposed to be me someday? This prompted me to evaluate my inner self and my future growth and direction. We move forward and grow with our career, but are we intentional about our inner legacy, of how others will remember us?

Let's go back to the first ten years of my career in the financial services/ credit card industry in the '80s. Business deals were done by playing golf with men. On the course, you would talk and negotiate the contracts to sign later. Friendships and trust with the people you would conduct business with and partner with were developed. During these years, the core of my business sense was evolving in my professionalism of character, wit, and knowledge to win the deals. I was creatively learning to think outside the box of the traditional man's world to win the big deals. My mind was working as my father taught me—the engineer's mind of the chess game. Every move has a consequence and goal in the end game, don't forget that. What does the finished project look like? Work back from that. At this time, women played golf or we would lose a seat at the table for contract opportunities. I learned to play both games at the same time.

The game of golf soon turned into sitting in cold water duck blinds and walking pheasant fields to sign contracts with men in the hunting industries. As relocations happened for my family, I was exposed to different industries and opportunities. My industries changed, but the principles of the games were the same: lots of men and standing my ground. Did my career harden and shift down the gentle soul that I might have inherited?

Am I that legacy, or can I be that legacy in my career world of business ownership and male-dominated industries?

I am deep in the politics of the world of business ownership and growing my business. There's nothing about a gentle soul in that . . . Or is there? Standing my ground, could it be that I have tenacity, and GRIT? Could GRIT also mean having a gentle soul, but being more direct and out there with accountable actions?

Does having a gentle soul mean you are weak in business? Could it be that under my other qualities these days in business, the gentle soul has been evolving within me so that I might be described as *an authentic person who is approachable and dependable, trustworthy, and a friend to many?*

From the past years of experiences, could my mindset of business environments also bring the characteristics and the inside soul of the person I know I am today to merge with the "gentle soul" many generations ago would have described? Or do we get hardened by the world and the actions of others in our everyday lives? Are we torn by the reality of being wives, mothers, caretakers, and peacemakers in a world of constant negotiations, contracts, and defending our knowledge? Has professional success hardened us as women in business and at home?

This is my challenge of growth today. Women are the leaders and influencers of our children and the people we work beside daily. Are we watering others to bloom and grow from our own experiences and knowledge of balance in business and family life? Let's evaluate what we pass along. Let's not pass along the weeds. We are in a society and world where the weeds have not been pulled and the ground is hard. A good gardening and tilling are in order to refresh and bring new growth to ourselves and to the many people we encounter daily. We are all born to grow, but not solo or in a silo of one. Begin by dusting your own dirt off and pulling the unwanted weeds. Do some soul-searching today.

How are you growing these days, and what soul are you putting out there to be remembered by? Are there characteristics that have changed you over the years that need to have a "goose egg hit on the head" shockwave to invite you to change? Do some of us need to wake up and appreciate who we are, where we are, and what we have accomplished? Do we appreciate the growth and tenacity we have, and all the layers of our soul that are yet to be discovered, that make up who we are? Our DNA and environment have made us who we are, to this point. We can stay true to our upbringing and how we are wired, and accomplish the world of business maneuvering, if we support each other in the growth of our souls. It's not just a gentle soul that raises the kids and builds a business; it's also our kindness and compassion while being authentic to others.

We juggle many balls, have many demands daily, but who are you striving to be on the inside? Let's not get lost on the outside stuff. We can all change our perspective and know it's possible. Nothing is easy, but many things are possible with lots of work and GRIT.

I'm a work in progress; we all are until we are six feet under. We all get caught up in our families, school, careers, and today's busy world of technology and travels. Evaluate your own growth. Give yourself a report card every now and then. Look back for just a second, knowing you can't change your past, and then turn your attention forward. What's the business plan for yourself? There's a world of opportunity for careers and business deals every day.

I have relocated many times, expanded my knowledge in multiple careers, and have friends I cherish from state to state. I have gotten caught up and stumbled in life and business and have also fallen so hard I couldn't breathe some years. Here's some of my hard-earned advice:

- Stop, reflect before you get into your world of the busy, busy, busy and other people's hardness around you, and find your inner *joy*.

- Spend some time on a front porch with neighbors, invite friends over for cards and tea (or tequila if it's me), and find *joy*.

- Let your kids play and explore together outside of the technology world. How do we teach our kids to stop? You start by setting the example. Get out of the carpool lane and walk up to visit with a friend or make a new one. We've got this if we put intention and time to it. We help each other grow.

We've got this, ladies—and gentlemen too!

I'm off to continue my journey every day. The months following my mother's death might have been a spirit crusher for me, but as my husband, Steve, reminded me, it didn't reach my soul. I thank him and others who have been through journeys of growth with me for reminding me of this. I'll till my foundation with the "gentle soul" reminder of the legacy I might leave someday.

I wish you all joy and finding your soul every day, whatever that may be.

Jeanie Brewster carries a Bachelor of Science degree in Marketing that has served her well with opportunities in multiple industries and regions for the past thirty-plus years. Starting her career as one of the first fifty employees of Discover Card Financial Services, she was subsequently instrumental in transforming the outdoor hunting industry for duck hunting to *Super Retriever Series* on ESPN. Following Jeanie's move to Kansas City, her career spanned from NASCAR races to launching the national certification for women-owned businesses for the region. She is known for being authentic and directly getting to the point of the situation and outcome. Her career experiences have ranged from diversity and inclusion to advancing business issues and to being a community advocate for children's rights and health.

If Jeanie is not serving her community or volunteering, you can find her cooking, finding her Julia Child mojo!

Jeanie is a Kansas tornado native who landed in Saint Louis in 2019.

www.linkedin.com/in/jeaniebrewster/

Sheila Buswell

No Syllabus for Life

Through a life that has taken me down unexpected paths, I have learned that things take longer than expected, and they are often not as they appear. I learned a lot on my journey through school and in the military. Here are some lessons I learned along the way.

I grew up in Dugway Proving Ground, a military testing base in the west desert of Utah. My dad worked there as a civilian after he retired from the army. Drafted out of college in the 1950s he made a career of the military and served in the Vietnam War. The day my dad left for Vietnam, my mom learned she was pregnant with her seventh of eight children. My mom is a tough lady, and she had a tour of duty of her own that year. Now that I've experienced deployment, I have a different view of military families. It is much easier to be deployed than to have a loved one deployed. My parents taught me how to learn and grow through all I experience.

If you asked me at eighteen if I would end up in the US Army, I wouldn't have believed it. I had it in my mind that people went to the army or went to jail. Now I know that people join the military for lots of reasons. In high school I graduated third in a class of twenty-seven. The valedictorian went to MIT; the salutatorian went to the Coast Guard

Academy; and then there was me. I got a scholarship to the University of Utah that I lost after the first year. Here's what happened:

A condition of my scholarship was that I needed to maintain a high GPA. I worked nights processing specimens for a national laboratory. I took classes during the day, and I slept when I could. After a while, my health and grades slipped. I had good grades the first quarter, but they declined after that. I was twenty years old and miserable.

One day, I went to class and tried to stay awake by sitting in the front middle seat. I fell asleep immediately. I am certain I was drooling. I woke with a start and knocked my books to the floor. The professor was leaving the classroom; I'd missed the entire lecture. That day was a turning point. While picking up my books and walking from class, I thought about how I wanted to see the world, and be physically fit, not tired and sickly. When looking for alternatives, I stumbled into the army recruiting office the next day.

During Basic Training and Advanced Individual Training, I met people from all walks of life. In my permanent duty station, I met my best friend. She is from Jamaica, and I am from Utah, yet we have so much in common. She is the only other person I know from my time in the military who left the military and completed their schooling.

I was assigned to a Forward Support Battalion, and we often went to the field for extended periods. When we returned, I went to our equivalent of Sbarro rather than eat in the army dining facility. We called it a DEFAC. After being in the field for fifty-three days, the idea of eating in the DEFAC was awful. My roommate ate at the DEFAC because she sent two months' pay home. She had no money until the next pay cycle, so she had to eat at the dining hall. I never sent my family money; I was always able to pay for anything. The military changed my definition of what poor meant. Before my time in the army, I defined poor as not spending money on designer jeans.

I received a medical discharge in 2001 after sustaining a foot injury in Bosnia in 1998. After my injury, I had to decide whether to exit the service at the end of my initial enlistment or to stay in the army long enough to get a medical discharge. My dad reasoned that I'd be better off to stay, and that I'd regret it if I didn't when there was another war. I said, "Dad, there is not going to be another war." He wisely replied, "There is always going to be another war!" I chose to stay on to get the medical discharge.

I continued my assignment in Germany. I was there, alone, for eight months. Being unfit for duty because of my injury, I had no job. I was in a holding pattern. This time in my life was mentally hard. By comparison, in Basic Training they had us run three miles every Thursday. One Thursday, we just kept going. We routinely ran six to ten miles on other days, but mentally we were only prepared for three, because that's what we expected on a Thursday. Most people fell out or stopped running. Those eight months in Germany were like that for me, mentally. I had prepared to Exit The Service (ETS) in May of 2000, so getting out almost a year later was tough. I finally ETS'd from the army on February 17, 2001, and went back to school as soon as I could.

This time, I was a different student. I had earned my place in the classroom. I was driven to finish what I had started long ago. I asked questions without fear. I didn't care if my classmates liked me. I was eager to learn. I talked to my best friend from the army daily. I realized professors were people, and I grew from our one-on-one interactions. I talked with one professor frequently. We discussed how engines and generators work. We both swam laps at noon, so we discussed kick turns and the proper timing of breaths during a stroke. Our conversation topics went from heat transfer and thermodynamics to roaches in the locker rooms. He brought bagels to class, but I remember his kindness for more than that. Though he has moved on to a different university, and I have made several changes in my professional career, I am still in contact with him today.

When I started work as an engineer at Anheuser-Busch, one of the few other women engineers told me to "try not to be so girly." I replied that I had "earned the right to act any way I wanted to." This woman was not ill-intentioned, but the idea that acting a certain way made someone a better engineer bothered me. I thought, "I've spent three-and-a-half years in the military, I completed my degree with good grades and good test scores, and I've been hired here as an engineer...I am qualified!" The adage "Don't judge a book by its cover" fit here.

My service in the military—what I viewed as a stepping-stone at the time—has become an important part of my identity. I use more profanity, sure, and I know the purpose of a bayonet. I problem-solve and figure out how stuff works. I am an awesome engineer because of the education I have and my military service; they are intertwined. The things I learned in school were expected, but much like my military service, every lesson was a surprise. Some lessons I didn't fully appreciate until years later. For instance:

I never understood why drill instructors stood so close to me until years later when a coworker tried to bully me. The project was to work on a design for plastic injection molding that I had created to solve a problem. I had no experience with this, so I was paired with a person who had years of plastic injection molding experience. The goal was to turn my designed part into a plastic injection molded part. Turns out, this person took my design and made the part, referred to it as his part, and refused to tell me how or why he made certain decisions. Instead of working with me, he tried to intimidate me by standing close to me. He was not scary at all, just big. I wasn't intimidated, but now I understood the lesson from my army drill instructors more than twenty years earlier. I didn't respond to him because I knew what he was trying to do. I calmly stepped away. He thought he could bully me, but it didn't work.

The army was not a destination or a career. For me, the army was how I was going to pay for college. To this day being defined as only a veteran bothers me, as my military service represents one part of what I have and hope to achieve. In my life, I trained for and ran two marathons; those always ended when expected. I always knew how long the marathon training runs would be. In life, though, like in the army, the training sometimes goes longer. The lesson learned in my longer-than-expected time in the army, and in my education, gave me the patience and perseverance to complete tasks when things don't go as expected. I don't judge things by how they first appear anymore.

All of us should look deeper than appearances and expect things to take longer than anticipated. If we're open to the lessons offered along the way, and break long tasks into smaller goals, we can achieve those goals and use them as a stepping-stone to our next achievement.

Sheila Buswell is the CEO and Cofounder of Buswell Biomedical. She developed the concept for the Upward Mobility in 2018 and started Buswell Biomedical with her husband, Gregg, in 2019.

Sheila attended high school in Dugway Proving Ground, Utah, graduating in 1995. After losing her scholarship to the University of Utah, she worked full time while attending classes full time for a year. In 1997, she joined the US Army, injuring her foot in Bosnia in 1998. After receiving a medical discharge in 2001, Sheila moved to Missouri to continue her education and to help her sister with babysitting. She earned a BS in Mechanical Engineering in 2005 from Missouri University of Science and Technology (then University of Missouri–Rolla). Sheila worked for Anheuser-Busch until 2007, then worked for DRS Technologies until 2010, where she met Gregg Buswell. Sheila holds an MS in Biomedical Engineering from Saint Louis University, conferred in 2015.

www.linkedin.com/in/sheilabuswellbiomedical/
www.buswellbiomedical.com
314-578-9953
sheila.buswell@buswellbiomedical.com

Jennifer Ono

Double Ds

The most pivotal moments in my life are the Double Ds: Diabetes and Divorce. These are the moments where I came face-to-face with situations that required me to grow when I didn't want to. Sometimes life gives us change even if we don't want it. Change happens, and sometimes it requires us to seek help to make it through.

At age thirty-three, I was living on my own and it was not in my plans to become a type 1 diabetic. This was the first life-changing event I had to navigate as an adult. I was employed by a nonprofit company that provided curriculum and reading support for children and teachers who were in low socioeconomic schools. Before I began this work, I had been a classroom teacher for six years: one in Chicago, four in Florida, and one in Missouri. At this stage in my life, I was single and focused on two things: my career and having fun. I had no attachments and was living my dream life: traveling all over the country working with children. I traveled five to six days a week across the United States and worked with amazing schools. One summer, the company hosted a national training in Baltimore, and some of my closest friends and mentors attended. It was like adult summer camp—we worked hard during the day and played hard in the evening. We were creating and innovating all the time, working to reach every teacher and assist in developing equitable reading opportunities for children. I was losing weight as I tried to shape up a bit for summer.

Toward the end of the two-week experience, we were having dinner together and I ordered my usual: coffee, water, soda, beer, and orange juice. I was on my second round of drinks before dinner arrived at the table. After dinner, my friend and mentor Tracy asked me how I was feeling and told me about her mother, who had diabetes. She said, "Drinking lots of fluids and losing weight can be symptoms. I am very worried about you. You need to see a doctor first thing as soon as you get home." I didn't think it applied to me, but I did call the doctor and set up an appointment for the day after I got home.

The doctor ordered a blood test, and I was shocked to find that my A1C blood sugar reading was 14.7 percent. Normal range is under 5 percent. The doctor diagnosed me with diabetes, prescribed pills to lower my blood sugar, and told me I needed to come back in the morning. I was stunned; however, I rescheduled some trips and went back in the morning to begin a new journey.

I called my aunt and cried and cried. I called my mom and dad to confirm if there was a family history of diabetes. We have an incredibly detailed family genealogy. There is no family history of diabetes at all. My faith in a higher power saved me that day. I wanted to go home, sleep, and not come out again. However, when I got home my kitten was meowing and needed food. Taking care of her made me get out of my own woe-is-me spiral. I felt like a robot, just going through the motions, but also knew my life wasn't over. It was going to change to a new normal, a life with shots, insulin, counting carbs, and being diligent about staying healthy. After starting insulin injections, I immediately improved. When you don't know you are sick, it can be hard to realize how bad you feel until you start feeling better. I read everything I could about diabetes and treatment. I went through a long period of wondering "Why me?" and making some bad food and life choices. Fast food restaurants were no longer my best friend and became an occasional acquaintance. I would take two steps forward and one step back.

Then, I started making choices that were better for me regarding food, sleep, and blood sugar control. I found a counselor who specialized in diabetes to help me adjust to this new life. I have now been a type 1 diabetic (T1D) for twenty-two years. This journey has been filled with ups and downs. It is daily adjustments and constant work to stay on top on my health. I have diabetic retinopathy, which is the beginning degradation of your eyesight and is a complication of diabetes. I already live with depression, and it has intensified since being diagnosed. I tell my amazing endocrinologist at almost every appointment, "If I were just a type I diabetic, I would be the best damn diabetic you would ever meet! But I am also a mom, teacher, robotics coach, daughter, friend, doctoral student, Scout mom, and, well, obviously overcommitted." I wouldn't change any of it, however, because it gives me an empathetic perspective on life that I would not have had otherwise.

Divorce is the second D and was more devastating and required more introspection and help to work through. As I was struggling with accepting and managing my diabetes in those early years, I took a different position with our company. I moved into a supervisory role and relocated to Hawaii. This change came with additional responsibilities and, wonderfully, a chance for me to limit my travel, which would be a benefit to eating, sleeping, and health. I loved the people, the culture, the change, everything about being in Hawaii. I adapted well, was a sponge for knowledge, and immersed myself in everything. It quickly became my adopted home.

I didn't dream about traditional milestones the way some people do. I had pie-in-the-sky dreams, like adopting special needs children who were about to age out of the system. I met my husband a year after relocation, and we were inseparable. Both of us were a bit older, and we forged our own path. I never really thought I would get married or have children, so I didn't have any plan. I did not know, with my age and my T1D, if I would be able to have children, so when we were engaged, we started trying for a child right away. Surprise! We quickly had a wedding and a baby girl. These were the two greatest moments of my life. I was lucky to have the opportunity to be a stay-at-home mom. Our son was born two years later, and our family was complete.

In the abstract, marriage is good, exciting, hard, passionate, and sad. Our marriage couldn't withstand our individual growth, however, and became unhealthy. The kids loved their dad, but even their relationship was strained. I asked for a divorce after trying everything, including counseling. Being with my children, though, meant the world to me. All I asked for was the freedom to move and take custody of the kids. He agreed, even though we wound up having to stay in the house together until the divorce papers were signed. This situation was awkward and painful and went on for six months. Thankfully, my parents hired a lawyer for me. She was my savior. She saw that we needed to leave and worked hard to get us what we needed financially. The kids and I landed in St. Louis, Missouri, with all our belongings and our seventy-pound chocolate lab. We moved into my parents' basement and recuperated.

No one gets married thinking it won't work or that it will end poorly. When it doesn't succeed, for some it can be amicable, and for some it is not. For me it was devastatingly painful. I was able to get through this time because I buried myself in the kids and alcohol. I am still working on unpacking the divorce with my therapist. My advice:

5. If it feels wrong, it probably is.

6. Don't let fear hold you back.

7. Let the right people love you.

Most of the time, I don't revisit that time in my life unless I am thinking about the kids, and don't get me started on how men and women post-divorce have very different expectations put upon them. Moving back in with your parents in your forties with two kids is, well, not the biggest esteem boost. Yet, being back with my mom and dad turned out to be the best place to be. The minute we arrived in St. Louis, I found therapists for myself and the kids. I knew we all needed someone impartial to talk with, and to help them where I couldn't. I also made sure that we joined a church to add another layer of healing and support. I still have residual effects from the divorce and the gaslighting that I endured, but therapy and facing reality have helped. In fact, very recently I realized that when anyone says to me, "You didn't tell me that," when in fact I know I did, I am transported into an angry, sometimes blind rage. This response is from the damage of living with gaslighting. It is not the current person or situation; it is leftover. This kind of epiphany has been a big part of my recovery from the Divorce D.

After growing through these life-altering events, I made it through by therapy, faith, and family. Now the updated Double Ds are Dancing and Dreaming of the future.

"You will always grow through what you go through."
– Tyrese Gibson

Jennifer Ono is the product of a family full of educators and considers herself a lifelong learner. She has recently coauthored and published a research methods article in conjunction with her doctoral program at Webster University in Missouri. In addition to an exemplary history as a classroom teacher for which she was awarded Teacher of the Year in 2018, Jennifer has experience in project development, educational consultation, and curriculum design. She has worked with a variety of students from young children to adults. She has taught and worked in multiple states across the country including Florida, Hawaii, Illinois, and Missouri. Jennifer's current educational passions include linguistic, racial, and cultural equity in the classroom and in life. She has two amazing children, Victoria and Wilson, and a small zoo of pets including: Velvet the lizard, Gorg and Ora the snakes, Miyaku the kitten, Gary the hedgehog, and Hershey the dog.

sites.google.com/kirkwoodschools.org/jennifermono/home
www.facebook.com/jennifer.ono
twitter.com/jo1229

Carla D. Bailey

Developing a Growth Habit

"Develop a passion for learning. If you do, you will never cease to grow."

Growth! Everybody says they want it, but not everybody wants to invest the time and effort it takes to grow. What about you? Are you willing to do what it takes to experience optimal growth in your life? Growth is the gap between your present and future self that leads you to your best self. Let's face it, growth is not easy, but the gain from growing is greater than the agony of the process. You have to endure great sacrifice to experience great growth, which requires a strong commitment. Our growth is not something we can afford to leave to chance while only taking occasional actions. Developing a growth habit comes through intentional and consistent practice of regular engagement in growth actions, behaviors, and experiences that stretch you beyond your current capabilities. For me, growth has never been optional. It has been a habit that I have intentionally developed throughout my life. The personal growth that has happened in my life results from consistently developing a habit of living outside of my comfort zone and daring myself to stay within the growth zone.

Since I was a young girl, I have been ambitious, curious, driven, confident, and constantly pushing myself to accomplish things I have never done before. Growing up, we had a basketball court in our backyard. I admired my two older brothers, who were great at basketball. They made it look so easy. I am sure it helped that they were both tall. While I was not nearly as tall, I was determined to be as good as they were, which was wishful thinking. They did not believe I could achieve this goal because I did not play basketball. I would go to the backyard every day after school and practice shooting the ball in the basketball hoop. I failed lots of times. However, for years I kept going back to the backyard each day to practice. While my brothers would never agree that I am as good as they are, I became a pretty good shooter.

As a child, I never listened to people telling me what I could not do, even if it was something I had never achieved. My parents often share stories with my two children of how when others would tell me what I could not do, instead of hanging around trying to convince them otherwise with my words, I was too busy running off proving them wrong with my actions. Where did this fearlessness come from? My faith and my parents. I am grateful to have been raised by wonderful parents who instilled in me a strong faith and the confidence to firmly believe that I could do all things through Christ who strengthens me.

Many years ago, when I entered the world of work as a young professional, I approached my career with the philosophy that comfort was a threat to my growth, which meant I had to be willing to stay uncomfortable. Throughout my career, I deliberately sought out and took advantage of opportunities that stretched me. I intentionally raised my hand early and often said yes to new opportunities, especially the scary ones. Growth occurred when I was challenged, not when I was comfortable.

In my first human resources (HR) job, I was both excited to work within my desired field and eager to grow. After one year, I decided to pursue the Society for Human Resource Management (SHRM) Certification, which gives you credibility as an expert in the HR field. My older, more experienced HR colleagues thought I was crazy for pursuing such an ambitious goal as a newbie. I recall the sarcasm in one of my colleague's voices when they asked, "Why would you choose to do such a thing so early in your career?" While it is not good communication skills to answer a question with a question, my witty nature could not resist. I replied, "Why have you not done such a thing so late in your career?" Annoyed, they made some excuses and walked away. I came to see that many of my older colleagues had years of continuous service in HR but not years of continuous growth. I vowed my career would be one of continuous growth, regardless of support from others.

In life, if I had waited to do things until I had the support of others, I never would have accomplished all the growth that I have. I always say, "If you wait until, then you never will."

When the pandemic suddenly hit in March of 2020, it brought much uncertainty into my life. Many things I could not control, but my growth was one of the things I could. I asked myself, "How can I grow and become better during the pandemic?" I wanted to evolve spiritually, personally, and professionally. So I embraced the discomfort and got busy consistently practicing daily growth actions and behaviors needed to achieve my desired results.

Two months prior to the pandemic, I decided to leap into a new personal growth experience. I was excited for my acceptance into the Executive MBA (EMBA) program at the Olin School of Business at Washington University in St. Louis. This was much more than pursuing another degree. It was a strategically chosen growth journey for deeper learning, stretching, and evolving into more of the unstoppable me God created me to be.

Unfortunately, the pandemic presented a million little reasons to abort this mission: major unanticipated delays to the start of the EMBA program; the entire twenty-month schedule; my two children suddenly becoming full-time virtual learners; my husband and I working remotely; and the EMBA graduation would now conflict with my daughter's high school graduation. Bummer, but I never back down from a challenge.

Why willingly put myself through a rigorous and intense growth journey with an already hectic family lifestyle in the midst of a pandemic? I believe no one can give out of an "empty well." As an executive transformational leadership coach, speaker, and learning and organizational development consultant for more than twenty-five years, I am still committed to keeping my well full, which is essential to my effectiveness in inspiring and developing leaders.

Those who know me know I am an intentional learning leader who is committed to continuous growth and becoming better. They have watched me devote my entire life to a habit of living outside my comfort zone. Developing a growth habit has been an interesting but wildly rewarding journey filled with many thrilling and scary leaps, through which I grew and became better. Growth has not always felt good *to* me, but it has always been good *for* me.

I know for sure: growth is hard. Unfortunately, many people do not like doing hard things. Honestly, I do not like doing hard things either. However, I intentionally choose to do hard things because I understand that there are some growth and rewards that only come because of having done the hard things. It is a myth that you must like doing hard things to do them. Truth is, even if we do not like doing hard things, we can still do them. Say this affirmation out loud with me: "I am capable of doing hard things!"

Growth matters. Your growth is a valuable differentiator; it is your superpower that uniquely positions you to succeed. Growth always requires you to let go of something. I get it. Letting go is difficult, but the pain of remaining the same is even more difficult. Letting go of comfort is a must to grow. It takes courage to step out of your comfort zone, but it takes commitment to stay out and not run back.

The fact that you are reading this book indicates you are ready to evolve and develop a growth habit. Kudos! When you develop the habits of growth, then growth will become a habit. Developing a better habit will lead to better growth. Imagine how radically different your life could be in six months to a year if you decided today to give yourself fully to your growth. You would transform into your better future self! Keep daring to unleash more and to live unstoppable in life and business as God has called you to do.

Lessons I Learned From the Growth Habit

1. **Growth takes Guts**: Be courageous, confident, and fearless. Be gutsy in your growth.

2. **Growth requires Grit**: Be passionate and persistent in putting in the effort and consistently doing the work daily. Be disciplined.

3. **Growth requires Grace**: Give yourself the grace to grow, to fail, to make mistakes, and to grow at your own pace.

Coaching Reflection

1. Do I approach my personal growth as a habit or with randomness?

2. What mindset or behavior shifts do I need to make to consistently grow?

3. What growth and transformation am I denying myself by not developing this habit?

Growth Habit: Three Practical Strategies

1. **Shift From Comfortable to the Uncomfortable**: Get uncomfortable and push yourself out of your comfort zone to grow. Stay curious and open to new experiences.

2. **Practice Growth Daily:** Habits are formed in your daily routine. Schedule time daily to practice and regularly engage in growth actions and experiences.

3. **Grow in the Dark**: Life has dark days, but do not quit. Focus not on the discouragement from the darkness but on the opportunity to grow into better.

Carla D. Bailey is a highly sought-after professional speaker for her inspiring, engaging, and revelatory messages on transformational leadership and growth. She is passionate about helping leaders, especially women leaders, uncover and unleash their inner greatness to live unstoppable in business and life. For more than twenty-five years, she has been helping leaders achieve their full potential by coaching, facilitating, and speaking on leadership. Carla has extensive experience as a human resources business executive, consultant, and learning and organizational development professional. She is a certified executive coach. In addition to owning her business, she serves as the head of learning and organizational development for Washington University in St. Louis.

Carla was named the 2018 Association for Talent Development St. Louis Professional of the Year. She is involved in community service and serves on local boards. When not speaking and coaching, she enjoys traveling and new experiences with her husband, William, daughter, Nalini, and son, Noah.

www.instagram.com/carladbaileyww/
www.facebook.com/CarlaDBaileyWorldwide
www.linkedin.com/in/carla-d-bailey-eccp-485a2613/

Sarah O'Sullivan

Lessons from Bolivia

Our small Cessna plane landed with a bone-jarring thump. I held my breath as the plane shook aggressively across a dirt runway as we came to a stop. I looked out the window and saw a small, colorful two-story wooden building. I was told this was the airport. We had just arrived at Rurrenabaque, a small town in the heart of the Bolivian rainforest. Seventeen hours of travel and three airports later, I realized my adventure had just begun.

We collected our bags, piled into a van, and started our two-hour drive down a rugged dirt road to the Rio Colorado boarding school. An hour into the drive, there was a flat tire due to the poor road conditions. We stopped in a very remote area to change the tire by flashlight. I felt anxious and vulnerable as I looked out into the complete darkness. I knew I was a long way from home.

Once we arrived at the school, we settled into the small one-story building where we would be staying the next couple weeks, sleeping in bunk beds under mosquito nets. The boarding school was composed of small one-story brick buildings with thatched roofs, screened-in open windows, and concrete floors. Roughly two hundred and fifty students dressed in white-and-blue school uniforms attended the school, where most stayed during the week since they lived too far to commute back and forth daily.

For the previous six months, our Engineers Without Boarders (EWB) student chapter worked diligently with the community to design and engineer improvements to the school. The main mission of the partnership was to provide running water for the school, including clean drinking water and showers.

I was part of a smaller team assigned to assess the water at the school and nearby communities by completing health surveys and water testing to establish a community health baseline. My group consisted of my friend Zach from the EWB student chapter; Claudia, a Spanish/English interpreter; and two students from the boarding school, Daniella and Alvarado, who interpreted from Spanish to the local indigenous dialects, Aymara and Quechua.

At our first stop, a middle-aged woman and a boy approached us. The boy was only about seven years old and carried a machete. Neither were wearing shoes, and I could see half-inch gaps in between the boards of their small wooden home. I asked the mother where they get their drinking water, and she took me along a path through the jungle to a brown, cloudy stream where I collected samples. My heart dropped knowing this was the water they drank from. I wished right then and there that we could offer them a better, more immediate solution.

Farther down the road, we approached a hand-dug shallow well shared by a group of homes. The well was covered with a handful of boards to keep large rodents and pests out. However, there were gaps in between the boards large enough to allow bats a place to hang from and slumber. The well smelled heavily of guano. I thought back to my first EWB meeting where I learned animal feces is a major contamination source for surface water, which contributes to diarrhea and a high child mortality rate.

At another stop, a woman told me they walked forty-five minutes every day to the nearest stream to collect their water. When I asked how she felt about her water quality, she smiled and responded, "Oh yes, we like having water." I thought to myself, "I can turn on a faucet in my house at any time I want for clean drinking water, and this woman is happy to walk forty-five minutes to collect some, regardless of the quality. How many times a day must she make that trip?"

We spent all day driving up and down the main road, stopping at each group of houses to speak with families. When we arrived at the home of our interpreter Daniella, we were offered fried rice cakes with cooked meat, eggs, and carrots inside. Her family home was a small, open one-room building with a dirt floor. I was nervous to eat the food since I was not sure how it was prepared but didn't want to insult our hostess's gracious hospitality. I was also hungry, and the food smelled and ultimately tasted delicious!

By the end of the first day, we realized we did not bring enough bottled water along for our day's trip in the humid heat. As we grabbed water samples from a well at one of our last stops, an older, kind, gentle woman could see the exhaustion and thirst on our faces. She picked an armful of fresh oranges from the tree in her yard and offered them to us with a warm smile, wanting nothing in return. There was something about her smile. No words were necessary. She was just happy to help us on our way. We were all very grateful to her. I could tell she had a kind soul. She reminded me of my own grandmother.

The families we met had so little compared to the everyday things we are accustomed to and take for granted in the United States, and yet were altruistic, generous, and overflowing with community warmth and love. The people I met were some of the most selfless and giving people I have ever encountered. They were especially welcoming to us even though we were strangers. So many smiled, waved, and tried to make jokes with us even though we didn't fully understand one another due to the language barrier. Time slowed down. There was no hustle and bustle or distraction from electronics. The nearest police were hours away in Rurrenabaque, but there was no crime. People in each community took care of one another before themselves. One family gifted me a wooden hand-carved bow and arrows used to hunt howler and spider monkeys from the trees, the same kind their ancestors had used for generations prior. I still have it to this day. Looking at it makes me smile, remembering my time in Bolivia and the kindness of its people.

Despite being from the other side of the hemisphere, with different languages, ideologies, and cultures, we were able to connect with the students and members of the community on a deep level. I witnessed firsthand that people are very much the same. They experience the same range of emotions and share the same spirit no matter where they live. All people have the same basic needs, like the need for clean drinking water. As a mother myself, I can see that all mothers want the same for their children: health and happiness.

I will never forget the bonding moments we shared with the students. They were so simple, yet impactful, like when we played soccer, or taught the young girls songs and dances from our childhood like "Little Sally Walker" and "The Hokey Pokey," while we laughed and danced to the games they taught us.

We embraced their rich culture by attending the Mother's Day festival at the school, where the students dressed in traditional Bolivian clothing full of color and performed customary dances. A small group of us were also fortunate enough to attend a church service in a small one-room building in the community. Despite the language barriers, we joyfully sang to God, unified by the greater power that brought us all together.

Before venturing on this trip, I knew the community did not have access to clean water outside of a few hand-dug shallow wells. Nonetheless, seeing firsthand how it affected the community's health including young children—without immediate access to rudimentary health care—left me crushed.

This experience made me grateful, humbled, and honestly a bit ashamed for having ever complained about minor inconveniences. To say it was life-changing would be an understatement! I had signed up with EWB for the chance to travel internationally and experience new cultures. However, this trip gave me so much more. I left having grown as a person, where the community impacted me more than I could have ever impacted them.

Through this experience, I learned that growth happens when:

- You are open-minded and try new things.
- You step outside your comfort zone and experience trials and tribulations, where you learn through failures and mistakes.
- You have the courage to not quit and keep moving forward, even if your brain tells you lies like "I can't" and "I'm not enough."
- You put in the work. "There are no shortcuts to any place worth going." – John Maxwell.
- You stay grateful.

I've also learned my personal fulfillment comes from using my talent and skills to serve others and to try and make a positive impact.

After ten years in the workforce, I started my own company, Montero Construction Services, named after another city in Bolivia. I loved the strength of the name. By choosing a name connected to Bolivia, I will always be reminded of my purpose and passion, both of which I found through my journey: helping others. During my Bolivia trips, I experienced true servant leadership, where people in the community took care of one another before themselves. Since then, I have tried to carry this principle with me as a servant leader.

Sarah O'Sullivan is the founder of Montero Construction Services, LLC, a certified woman-owned business enterprise offering project management, engineering, and environmental compliance services.

Prior to founding her own company in 2021, Sarah worked for both Fortune 500 and start-up consulting companies, serving a variety of industries including agricultural, manufacturing, mining, construction, water and power utilities, and the Department of Defense. She was also Regional Environmental Manager for a Fortune 50 company. She is a licensed professional engineer and holds a bachelor's degree from the Missouri University of Science and Technology (Missouri S&T) in Rolla, Missouri.

Sarah is a member of numerous professional organizations and is passionate about serving others and improving communities. She currently volunteers with the St. Louis Gateway Professional Chapter of Engineers Without Borders.

Sarah loves to travel and enjoys sports, yoga, the outdoors, and spending time with her husband, Tom, and two daughters, Abigail and Madelyn.

Sosullivan@monterocon.com
www.linkedin.com/in/sarah-o-sullivan-pe-pmp-9a191530/
www.facebook.com/profile.php?id=100080379672797
www.monterocon.com

Colleen Filla

Grow Through What You Go Through

OK, friend, here is the truth: I did not know if I could tell my story in this book. Who am I amongst all these other amazing women? I am only a stay-at-home mom who tutors kids in reading. I almost missed this opportunity, but I realized it is important that I own my story. Probably some of you feel the same way. No matter where you are in life, everyone has a story to be told, and it deserves to be heard.

I am the youngest of four children. And by youngest, I mean youngest by a bunch. By the time I was in seventh grade, all my siblings had completed college, started their careers, and gotten married. I felt I couldn't be the one child in my family who didn't succeed. My parents had high expectations, but the biggest pressure always came from within me. I pushed myself to set goals and accomplish them on my own.

Throughout my school career, I earned pretty good grades, sought out leadership opportunities, and traveled to experience different cultures. With hard work and effort, I accomplished most of my goals. I graduated with my bachelor's in psychology, earned a master's in special education, took a position as a special education teacher, and got married. Life was moving quickly and going smoothly.

When my husband and I decided to start a family, I learned the hard lesson that sometimes you grow in ways that are not of your own choice.

We were successful in getting pregnant after just a few months of trying. Unfortunately, I had a miscarriage. My doctor said that my cycle would be off for a bit, so when my cycle didn't come the next month, I wasn't surprised. I started feeling sick, though, so my husband suggested I take a pregnancy test. I thought he was crazy. Turns out he was right! A healthy baby boy arrived that spring.

When we tried again to get pregnant two years later, we thought it would be just as easy. I had miscarried once, but that can be common. We told our parents excitedly, and I called the doctor to make my eight-week appointment. I would not make it to that appointment. I had another miscarriage. We would try again, get pregnant, and then another miscarriage. We were heartbroken. I wanted answers. I was helpless and stuck in a limbo of sadness.

I could not handle seeing my friends' happy, healthy little babies all over my social media pages, so I left. I held my baby boy a little tighter but could no longer read certain children's books or sing certain songs to him. They would hit my heart too strongly, especially the song, "You Are My Sunshine." The verse about waking from the dream without a loved one was too much to take.

I felt so very alone. I did not feel my husband could fully understand my heartbreak. He did not have to both physically and emotionally experience the miscarriages. I felt like it was somehow my fault.

With folic acid supplements and other suggestions from the doctor, we began trying again, a bit hopeful that we had found the problem and a solution. Unfortunately, a few weeks later I had another miscarriage. I totally fell apart this time. It was just too much.

I kept all my fertility issues mostly to myself. At work, I was friendly and talkative but never let anyone in too closely. The day after my fourth miscarriage, I dragged myself into work. My amazing co-teacher took one look at my face; she could see right through my wall and asked me what was wrong. I did not want to say the words out loud because if I did, I wouldn't be able to hold it together any longer. It would be too real. From somewhere deep inside I got the words out. She told me, "I'm so sorry," and gave me the biggest, tightest hug. I felt all the love, warmth, and comfort that I needed in that hug. Letting myself fall apart and be open with more people helped me heal. Unfortunately, my co-teacher lost her battle with ALS a few years later. Her love remains and always will. The warmth of that hug can still carry me through a hard day.

My doctor recommended a fertility specialist. The night before our appointment, I was lying on the floor, crying. I couldn't get up. My heart had nothing left to give. Filled with despair, I had lost hope. With my husband's love and support, I made it to the appointment. I was shocked that the doctor had answers for us, with a very simple solution. I held my breath the entire pregnancy, not able to fully accept it.

Nine months later we welcomed our second little boy into the world. Holding him in my arms, I finally smiled and sighed with relief. I was once again a mother, but I was a different person from when I held my first son in my arms. I will always carry with me that I have more babies in heaven than I do on earth.

While all of this was going on, a lot had changed at my work too. I was assigned to teach more and more students at a time, which made it extremely difficult to provide the strategic individualized instruction that each student deserved. My boss, who supported but also challenged me to grow as a teacher, had moved on to a new position. I also had the amazing experience of co-teaching with a general education teacher. These were the best years of my teaching career. We both thrived from collaborating, and our students benefited. When we were told that the school district was no longer supporting co-teaching at the elementary level, it was heartbreaking.

After maternity leave, I was no longer co-teaching, and I felt stretched thin and unsupported. I had a baby and toddler at home, and my husband was traveling for work more than ever. I was not growing, or even keeping afloat. I was drowning. I wasn't the teacher I wanted to be, nor was I able to be fully present at home. My job left my tank empty at the end of the day. Something had to give. I finally came to the heartbreaking decision to walk away from my dream job. But I knew in my heart I would teach again, somehow.

Fast-forward a few years, and the pandemic hit. I was a stay-at-home mom with my now three boys and enjoying being their first teacher, but something was missing. A former coworker told me she was enjoying tutoring using a great reading program. Always up to learn something new, I chose once again to grow as a teacher. I took the leap and began tutoring online. I liked it so much I decided to start my own company, Empowering Readers Tutoring. I am so thankful for those who have helped and supported me in finding a way to be present for my family and to follow my dream of teaching. I am back to my roots and passion of helping my students to learn and grow.

My experiences of multiple heartbreaks on my personal and professional rollercoaster helped me grow emotionally. I am now a more empathetic and understanding person. We never really will know what is going on in another person's life. Many people had no idea what my husband and I were going through. Now, if I struggle with another person, I try to look deeper. I also learned it is impossible to always make it through life on my own. It isn't weakness to need to lean on others to make it through. It takes a strong person to admit when they need help. You may have to lean on your community to get through a tough time, but there is good stuff that lies ahead.

Be that ear that listens. Give that hug to someone who needs it. It could be powerful enough to last a lifetime. Hold on tight to your community; you never know when you will need them most. Do not make yourself smaller. Stand tall for who you are today, and always be open to grow. You are worthy. Own your story!

Colleen Filla is a special education teacher and reading specialist who runs a private online tutoring practice, Empowering Readers Tutoring LLC. In her teaching, she works with students to provide them with the tools to be successful learners and readers. She believes in helping students not only to grow their academic skills but the person as a whole. She uses her background in psychology and special education to help her students develop a growth mindset toward learning and growing as an individual.

Colleen obtained her BA in Psychology and her MA in Special Education from Truman State University. She then earned her MA in Reading and her Reading Specialist Certificate from Webster University.

Colleen is married with three children. In her spare time, she enjoys being outdoors: hiking, gardening, taking pictures, and exploring our country's state and national parks.

empoweringreading@gmail.com
www.facebook.com/empoweringreaderstutoring

Dafna Revah

When Growing Means Slowing Down

On March 19, 2020, I had a flight to Tel Aviv for a much-needed vacation. I was looking forward to seeing family and friends whom I hadn't seen in over a year. I had plans to go to the beach, read a book—something I didn't have time for at home—and eat lots of good hummus and pita. Instead, I canceled the trip that morning after receiving hundreds of pandemic notifications. I was extremely disappointed, but I had no idea what was to follow. The next day, Israel closed its borders to all travelers, and I was relieved I wasn't stuck on an across-the-Atlantic flight at the time.

Almost immediately, starting March 22, 2020, orders came from different cities and states telling everyone to stay home and ordering the closure of businesses. I had to go into overdrive for work. We had to determine what stores could stay open, who could work, how they could work safely, and how we could reach our customers who were living in fear themselves.

The next few weeks were extremely hectic. I worked from home with my two-year-old son and with my husband, David, co-owner of our company, CBD Kratom. Every day, we updated our customers on what stores were open, got updates about the team, and responded to our customers who were reaching out to us on our new online chat that was open from eight a.m. to ten p.m., seven days a week. It was also the busiest

228

time of the year for us. April was coming, which meant it was time to celebrate. There is a cannabis holiday during the month that takes place every April 20, or rather 4/20. Since the year was 2020 and things were all kinds of sideways, we decided to celebrate the 4/20 holiday all month long.

At the time, we only had nine out of thirty-six stores open, so I was fielding lots of questions about online orders. We had more online orders in April 2020 than ever. Things were so busy with work since the first stay-at-home order that I didn't have any time to reflect on what was happening or what life would be like in the coming months.

Then, on April 25, 2020, I found out I was pregnant with my second child. I had so many emotions: happy, nervous, excited, but I was also scared. I knew this time would be different. I didn't know how I would handle my work responsibilities, parenting responsibilities, and all the new pressures from the pandemic. One of my best childhood friends was pregnant at the same time, and she detailed how scary it was to visit the hospital and how all those visits had to be done alone for safety precautions. I was scared about what this pregnancy would be like.

Honestly, the next couple of months were a blur. I was taking things day by day, holding down my nausea in the morning and evenings while still working from home and taking care of my family. The highlight of my week was visiting my grandma in her driveway. We'd do the hokey pokey and host puppet shows outside with my two-year-old, separated by at least six feet. My grandma has always been an inspiration to me, and I had to make sure I was still connecting with her during this time. Once I passed thirteen weeks in June, I started to feel better and came out of my mental fog.

Simultaneously, things began to take off at work. I was working on overdrive to keep the daily items running, while also working on the future. As stay-at-home orders expired, we started reopening stores, and David and I revisited the idea of opening stores in New York City. I went to school in Manhattan, and it was a dream of mine to open a CBD Kratom branch there. The city also met our requirements for a new market: foot traffic, population-dense, and void of quality cannabis/kratom retailers. But it's an expensive place to set up a business. It was a risk we were willing to take.

David and I had traveled to New York City for a national real estate conference in December 2019 to look for storefronts. After looking at more than fifty locations, we identified a location in Midtown Manhattan that we believed would be a prime CBD Kratom storefront. We started negotiating a lease, but with the pandemic, we stopped looking for new locations.

Though things in New York City were still not great in June 2020, David and I identified an unheard-of opportunity. With newly abandoned storefronts, many retail spaces were available for rent at low prices. We realized that if we were going to open in New York, the time was now.

We spent the summer months talking with our agent, planning out what areas we wanted to open in, and what would work best for us. Then, in September, we decided it was time to tour the stores. Since I was pregnant, I was advised not to travel. Up until that moment, I hadn't even thought about this massive change. Before the pandemic, I was traveling for work at least bimonthly. Travel had become a crucial part of our growth strategy, and I couldn't participate.

When we planned David's trip to New York, I became discouraged. I realized I needed time to understand how life had changed over the last six months. I needed to step back and understand my emotions. I couldn't travel, and I couldn't see the potential locations. I had to give myself space and compassion.

So while David and his brother drove fifteen hours nonstop on a Sunday, I stayed at home with my two-year-old and did nothing. No meetings, no answering emails, or even personal texts. We watched lots of television and played outside. I remember walking with him to the neighborhood park and feeling some relief. I finally had a chance to breathe. I was lucky to spend time with my son. It helped me process the idea of putting myself and my health first. It helped make way for my new reality.

When David returned from his trip, we signed our first New York City lease in late September 2020. With the pandemic still raging throughout the US, he reported that the streets in New York were empty, but I knew the city would come back. From St. Louis, we continued working on signing additional New York City leases and opening the storefronts.

Then I gave birth at the end of December and took some time off to be with my son. When I returned in mid-February, most of my efforts were focused on the new stores. We opened the Chelsea location on April 20, 2021, just under one year and one month after the first stay-at-home order was issued. I traveled to New York for the grand opening, which was my first work trip since the pandemic began. I was nervous about leaving the kids but so excited to see all the hard work come to fruition.

The new store looked so good, and the team was excited. Several news outlets came by to take pictures to celebrate the new store opening on the cannabis holiday. I realized that taking care of myself helped take care of the business. If I am not doing well, then I cannot do good for the business. I'm proud of the growth I have made in that department. It used to be work first, without regard for my personal needs. Now, I understand how the two are intertwined and that it's essential to take care of both.

As of May 2022, there are eight New York City CBD Kratom locations, and it is quickly becoming the best-performing market for the company. In 2021, I also helped the company expand to Philadelphia, where we now have three locations open. I continue to take care of myself and reflect on things. If I allow time to process my experiences, I'm more thoughtful and understanding. Now, I couldn't go back. Taking time for myself is central to the way I work, and to my company's success. I've left behind working all the time and always moving forward without assessing the past. My growth and my company's growth came from taking time for myself, and I recommend it to everyone.

Dafna Revah owns and operates the largest privately owned cannabis and kratom retailer in the United States, CBD Kratom. Revah serves as the company's vice president and manages the company's growth with a team of over four hundred and fifty employees. CBD Kratom currently has more than fifty locations in Chicago, Dallas, Houston, New York, Philadelphia, and St. Louis. Revah and her team are looking to continue growing the company and expanding to new cities in 2023. Revah is a former grant writer for the Jewish Federation of St. Louis and Audience Development Director at the *St. Louis Business Journal*. She is also a mother of two and was selected as *Greenway Magazine*'s One to Watch in 2020.

www.linkedin.com/in/dafnarevah/
www.instagram.com/dafna_revah/
www.facebook.com/dafna.revah

Beth Gunter

What Are You Afraid Of?

A mentor once shared a quote with me that I immediately took to heart, "Do one thing every day that scares you!" Frequently misattributed to Eleanor Roosevelt, it was first written by Mary Schmich, a *Chicago Tribune* columnist.

I've always hated being scared of things. Yet, through that fear, we find growth and strength. So, how do we handle it? Throughout my life, I've faced it head-on.

Have terrible stage fright? Join a Toastmasters group. Scared of heights? Let's do flying trapeze. Never performed on stage? Become a competitive (salsa) dancer. Public speaking? Take on a leadership role of an industry association where you emcee events. Afraid of being vulnerable with your creative passions? Write and publish a book. Worried about leaving your hometown? Move three thousand miles away for a job. That's what I did. By pushing yourself, training yourself to live in the uncomfortable, and doing something that scares you daily, you'll achieve the ultimate outcome—personal and professional growth.

At my all-girls high school in the Southeast, many role models and teachers supported and coached me. They instilled the belief that men and women have equal abilities and opportunities. While my classmates rolled their eyes at my numerous questions, my curiosity was sated. I volunteered, took many babysitting jobs to earn money to pay for my debate trips. Through that learning, I grew. That same curiosity has led me to success in my career.

Professionally, I've always taken the most challenging positions, such as leading a team that was nonexistent or not functioning at peak performance. The goal is to challenge myself and my team. Then, we grow together. I've led very successful teams who all achieved record-breaking numbers. It is nearly impossible to achieve success without creating a strong, collaborative team. Here are examples of employee experiences and how we achieved greatness:

Scenario A: "Flying under the radar." This employee had an incredibly smart and strong personality, and always had great excuses as to why they didn't make their numbers. They typically did just enough to get by. We had tough conversations about performance management. Those discussions are a bittersweet part of the manager's job. It's not fun to be tough, but it is incredibly rewarding when your employees rise to the challenge. I listened empathetically but didn't accept excuses. I held them accountable and asked probing questions: What's your plan to make up your numbers by the end of the month? What are your quick hits to have big wins? What do you have in the pipeline? How are you moving a client to a close? Together, we devised a plan to exceed expected performance.

Result: This employee contributed to a winning team, which won nationally recognized awards.

Scenario B: "Need a little guidance to be great." On one team, I inherited an employee who had a great relationship with their prior manager, resented me, and was underperforming. Over the next two years, we held regular meetings to build respect and rapport by demonstrating that I would roll up my sleeves and do the hard work to hit our numbers. We held each other accountable and had some of the toughest feedback sessions

I've ever experienced. For instance, they didn't want to be referred to as "my team" or "my employee"; rather, they wanted to be referenced as "the team" or "the employee." I changed my vernacular and demonstrated that I, too, was willing to learn and grow.

Result: Not only did this employee become a top performer and get promoted, but they also made me a more thoughtful manager.

Scenario C: "Top performer." The story of my top performer began with a rough first interaction. I conducted their new hire training, and this employee disrupted the class. I called them out by asking what they were discussing. In hindsight, this was too grade-schoolish, but even in that initial interaction, I could see there was greatness inside this person. People listened to them, were captivated by them, laughed at their jokes. In essence, they were a born leader. Throughout their career, I mentored and coached them, and polished off the rough exterior so that they weren't so salesy. Honest conversations helped get us there. We set stretch goals, and I pushed the right buttons to motivate them.

Result: They were always top of the leaderboards and helped others to learn from them to emulate and perform. They were instrumental in the team I led, winning multiple national recognition awards.

No matter what professional role, or where I lived, these guiding points have proven successful in my life:

Take on the biggest challenge. While it has inherent obstacles, taking on the underdog role with a team that needed the most work brings the tremendous rewards of a job well done.

Relationship building. My first management role was in small town South Carolina. My team increased branch sales by 129 percent in eight months. How did we do it? It wasn't rocket science; it was relationship building. Daily, I would be in the marketplace, the face of the brand, talking with people about what was important to them and how we had not delivered on those factors but would deliver them moving forward. The key was taking that commitment seriously and delivering on what we promised. The successes and connections were proven sustainable by the branch's continued record-breaking performance after my promotion.

Board of Directors. Get involved with boards where you are passionate about the organization's mission, and work with fellow board members who are well connected or affluent. Surrounding yourself with people who are strong examples of who you want to become is a great way to grow. Serving on boards for many years, I have not only gained deep friendships but also acquired many potential or new clients. Holding executive roles on volunteer boards has also been an important part of my leadership development. It is not easy to manage a volunteer board, to keep people engaged and retained. While boards are motivated by passion, people need to be compelled to be active, to support the cause, to raise money, and to give their time. If there is poor leadership on the board, people will inadvertently work against the organization's mission. These learned skills can also be applied to your paid management role, aka your "day job."

Collaboration. It's amazing how helping other divisions achieve their goals helps your team attain theirs. Living by the Golden Rule and building relationships internally to your team and externally within the organization always delivers great results. You never know when you will be working for someone you have supervised or worked with in the past.

Feedback. It doesn't always feel good, and people don't always welcome it, but make sure you are open to it and are able to provide constructive and appreciative feedback. A two-way experience, creating a safe environment for your employee to share how you can be better, will positively impact you as a manager and improve your team's performance.

Networking. Networking has been the number one way I have increased my professional influence. Helping people to improve themselves personally and professionally, with an added benefit of making some great friendships along the way, is deeply rewarding. Expanding your network is so valuable. You never know when you will come to a person's rescue, need a resource for business, or a job reference.

"Practice?! We talking about practice. Not a game…" Allen Iverson's infamous video about not attending practice is an ironic illustration of what can happen if people don't practice their craft. We don't want to believe it growing up, but it is true: practice makes perfect. Preparing for a client or an internal presentation, I write my thoughts down, watch myself present in the mirror, practice in front of my family, coworkers, video myself and play it back, etc. Why do I feel so strongly about practicing? Although I love working with people, public speaking still gives me pterodactyls in my belly. Practicing multiple times creates a sense of comfort and builds muscle memory for any presentation you give.

Be a nice human. This is a balance: how to be a nice human but still have gravitas as a leader. Honestly, what gets you to one level within your career and helps you relate to your employees may not be the behavior or persona you want to display in your C-Suite role. At the core of it all, if you are a nice human, your employees will know you care for them and will perform. "Remember, there's no such thing as a small act of kindness. Every act creates a ripple with no logical end." – Scott Adams

Through each role in my various careers, I get closer to my goal(s). At the age of twelve, while taking a rare road trip with my mom and sister, "Groove Is in the Heart" played on the radio and I decided to become President of the United States. I mapped out a path to achieve that lofty goal. While my goals have shifted, that same vision and determination helped me strategically take opportunities to increase my professional worth and my self-confidence to grow into more influential and challenging roles. The relationships I've made, and the communities I've been a part of, have made all the difference.

A trailblazer, risk-taker, and top performing salesperson and sales leader, Beth Gunter helps companies grow and improve performance. She has led teams in Charleston, Portland, and nationally. Beth recognizes that leaders can't accomplish their goals alone and loves developing high performing teams. She has an uncanny ability to hire outstanding talent and develop them into highly productive teams. She creates a culture of ownership, where employees take deep accountability and responsibility for not only their personal performance but also the team's.

In her current role as Chief Revenue Officer of a global publishing company, catering to K–12 teachers, Beth oversees the Press, Sales, Marketing, Professional Development, and Events business units. She has worked with a wide range of clients from Fortune 500 to insurance, health care, entertainment, education, and government. She holds a Women in Executive Leadership certification from eCornell.

Based in St. Louis and deeply involved in her community, Beth founded the St. Louis Networking event One Degree of Separation, which has realized over 250 percent growth in membership in over three years. She serves on several boards including the St. Louis Children's Hospital, Gamechanger Athletes, Gateway to Hope, and her alma mater Ashley Hall in Charleston.

www.linkedin.com/in/bethgunterstl/
www.instagram.com/virginia_line_publishing/

Lea Satterfield

Gratitude for Right Turns

When my two-year-old would say "that's not my plan" when asked to do something she didn't want to do, it made me reflect on how often I was using that phrase. I am notorious for thinking forward and working my way backward, thinking about what it takes to get from there back to where I am. I then focus my time and energy on those steps to reach my goals. I create plans and always have a vision for where I'm headed. When I think back, though, some of the most important moments of growth in my life were instances where my plan was to go left but life made me take a right turn instead.

Growing up in the '90s, the message was, "Stay in school, go to college, get good grades, and you'll have it all: wealth, security, a fun lifestyle and more!" If you had asked me at the end of high school what my aspirations were, I would have confidently stated, "I'm going to college to get a degree so I can go to law school to become an estate planning attorney."

My parents are great mentors. They were very supportive, and they challenged me. Political science was a common course of study for someone on the path to law school, yet my parents encouraged me to study something in my undergraduate work that led to a variety of employment opportunities if my plans changed, in case life happened. I landed in the Personal Financial Planning program at the University of Missouri–Columbia, which included a course on estate planning. I thought at least I would learn strategies to manage my own money smarter after college. Remember, I planned to have it all—because I was doing everything right.

Then life happened. I graduated from my undergraduate program in May of 2009 during the Great Recession. The job market was the worst it had been since the Great Depression. My plan was to stay in school, so you might be thinking I avoided the terrible job market. The competition was fierce to enter law school, and I needed to consider other law school options than at my alma mater. I didn't want to go anywhere else, and that made me question my drive for law school. I took a right turn when everyone else was taking a left. I went into the workforce.

While my professional life was transforming, so was my personal life. Building a relationship was not my focus. It was on building a career that would afford me what I wanted most: having the cool apartment in the "big city," which meant Kansas City to me at the time (I grew up in rural Missouri) and traveling. I was on a trajectory to be the "cool aunt," until a Thanksgiving family reunion changed my path.

My cousin, who is eight years my senior, and I were the only two girls on my mom's side of the family. I looked up to her. Our Thanksgiving tradition was to pile into her parents' house, have a big potluck meal at one p.m., and then go for a walk. We'd skip rocks in the river nearby, run and jump on the haybales, and throw around footballs if the weather permitted. A true Americana Thanksgiving.

The year she came back for the holiday with her six-month-old son was one I'll never forget. Stuffed from way too much food, I sat on a two-person love seat. She sat on the floor in front of me. As we talked, her son fussed. She changed him into comfortable clothes and swaddled him to soothe him. She looked at him with pure love on her face. That look changed me. I realized I wanted to experience that kind of love, and I realized I did want children of my own.

At the time I wasn't really living my dream. I had a terrible apartment and was barely making ends meet, and there was no self-afforded travel. So while I loved my work and had great colleagues, I knew I needed to make a change. Within six months after that Thanksgiving Day, I landed a dream job in Kansas City. The job would afford me the cool apartment downtown and the ability to have a ton of travel paid for by the company. I reconnected with friends who I grew up with, and they pushed me to join the online dating scene.

One site said most people find a long-term relationship with the sixth person they date online. Because of my experience with my cousin, I knew I wasn't casually dating. A quick coffee date was all I needed to determine if I wanted to get to know a person or not. My intuition was quick.

After nine months of online dating, the sixth person I was willing to meet was Mark, who is now my husband. We met for coffee on a beautiful April morning, which turned into lunch and then dinner the next night. I'm not sure I believe in love at first sight; but we both will say that as soon as we saw each other, we were completely at ease.

Mark and I have built a life we love most of the time. It's had some twists, like the "big city" I dreamed of living in turning into Los Angeles. We hiked the Incan Trail to Machu Picchu, which was Mark's top Bucket List item. With our two daughters, I have experienced the love I saw on my cousin's face. I'm grateful for that Thanksgiving Day, and to my cousin, for giving me the right turn I needed in my personal life. It led me to Mark and to this rich life we share.

After college and for over a decade after, I worked in the invest-ment regulatory space. I could get behind the mission, I got paid well, and overall had a good work-life balance (good time off, flexible work hours when needed, good maternity leave, etc.). I thought I was a "lifer," someone who was in for the long haul. I saw people come and go, but I didn't identify with the reasons why people left. I didn't expect the grass to be greener somewhere else, or the increased pay to be worth the increased responsibility, and so on.

Over the course of about six or eight months, though, my perspective started shifting. For instance, I could get behind the mission, but did I believe in the true impact of the work I was doing? I got paid well, but is money really everything? Did I really have good work-life balance if I was traveling three weeks a month while pregnant and with a child at home? I was starting to feel overextended, unseen, unsupported, and burned-out. My career was a huge part of my identity, though, so I felt like I had to hang onto it.

I remember one day, five months pregnant, walking into my oldest child's school. I had just ended one of the worst discussions of my professional career with a person in power at my company. A friend, who is a great friend now, was in the hallway. She took one look at me and tears came to my face, something an introverted, extremely private person would never do—cry in public. I realized I had become someone I didn't recognize. I realized that night that I had hung on as long as I could, and perhaps longer than was healthy. I realized life was too short to be that miserable professionally.

That was when I started dreaming and talking with those I trusted most and took a right turn. I now work with my mother, Dr. Thia Crawford, and provide financial education that is about more than building wealth; it's about building a happier, richer life. We support people to reach not only their financial goals but also their life goals. I knew what the research said about small businesses not making it, but I took a chance on me. I knew I needed to trust in myself and build something that I did truly believe in at my core.

Our business opened in early 2020, just as the pandemic was kicking into full swing. While I hope none of us ever live through a pandemic again, it opened a path from long before. I didn't start the business with the intention of diving heavily into estate planning, but due to the pandemic it became clear that I needed to study the current resources and information within the field for my own plan—to provide for my young daughters if the worst were to happen. As I was studying and building my estate plan beside Mark, our clients and partners were also craving the same knowledge. I now coach people through the process of creating a low-cost yet effective estate plan from start to finish.

As my path has changed, I've realized tough times don't define us, but instead we are defined by how we learn, make changes, and grow. At the end of our lives, we are more likely to regret the things we didn't try, versus trying things even if they don't turn out how we hope. I have no regrets. Those three right turns brought me full circle, and they are also three reasons my life today is richer than I could have planned. Life happened (and will happen again), and being open to growth has led me to a place where I couldn't be more thankful and grateful for the opportunity to be, have, and do what I want most.

Lea Satterfield, Founder and CEO of MPower Co, is a financial, well-being, and estate planning coach. It is Lea's personal mission to empower others to live a happier, more financially secure life. She is a trailblazer, along with her mother, Dr. Thia Crawford, in combining the fields of positive psychology and personal finance. Lea coaches people on finding contentment, gratitude, learning opportunities, and small goods—among other things—like she has learned to do to increase her overall sense of well-being.

Lea has been a lifelong learner in the field of personal finance: interning with the National Endowment for financial education in high school, earning a BS in Personal Financial Planning from the University of Missouri–Columbia, passing the Certified Financial Planner® examination, and completing an MBA with an emphasis in Business Finance from Arizona State University.

Lea is a wife, mom of two young girls, CEO, lover of Kansas City and Mizzou football, avid traveler, butterfly gardener, and pickleball enthusiast.

www.mpowerco.com
www.linkedin.com/in/leasatterfield/
www.instagram.com/mpower_finance/
www.facebook.com/MPowerFinance

Diane Finnestead MAT, Ed. S.

Who Will Hold My Hand?

Dedicated to Jayne Finnestead and Eddie Ellis

According to AARP, in 2020, fifty-three million Americans were unpaid caregivers to family members, up five million since 2016. One in three Americans today will need long-term care after the age of sixty-five, and with ten thousand Americans turning sixty-five every day as the baby boomers age, the number of unpaid family caregivers will only increase. How can we prepare for this need as a society and as individuals? What can be done to not just meet the needs of those we love but also grow into the best caregivers we can be for ourselves and our loved ones?

When I started in the long-term care insurance business in 1997, I had personal motivation; my former mother-in-law and my father-in-law were on the precipice of needing care, and lots of it.

Now, with more than twenty years in long-term care insurance, the biggest advantage for me personally as a caregiver and for my clients is, without a doubt, the fact that long-term care insurance reduces the emotional burden, guilt, and sometimes debilitating stress that comes with caring for a spouse and/or family member(s). It's quite a juggling act, and a big ask to become the unpaid caregiver in a family, because you don't know what the sacrifice will be nor the expectations. When one becomes the unpaid caregiver, it's usually an assumed role. The caregiver does the job out of love.

In my work, I collaborate with senior industry professionals as well as professional and nonprofessional family caregivers to offer free "Giving the Care Back to the Caregiver" classes/seminars in the community. I noticed patterns of behavior and similar emotions I had experienced when I had been a caregiver myself.

By conducting these classes, I observed and identified with two distinct behaviors found in the psychology behind caregiving: the theory of elasticity and the imposter syndrome. The theory of elasticity assumes that humans are like rubber bands and that as we stretch ourselves, we grow, yet we desire to be what we once were. We know there is a new normal, but the old normal is what we seek because that was and still may be our comfort zone. Like a rubber band, we reshape to what we were originally, though we might have few stretch marks. Our elasticity is what's being tested when we are thrown into situations that we're not prepared for, like when many of us—fifty million, in fact—are thrust into unpaid caregiving. We begin this journey by flying by the seat of our pants, spearheading the challenge, and synthesizing information and resources to become the unofficial "official" chief communicator in all family matters relating to the member needing care.

Often, a family member's evaluation of the caregiver's performance skills are subjective, and unsolicited opinions are not helpful and create stress. Not all unpaid caregivers are resilient enough to withstand the judgement of their loved ones. This scrutiny can lead to imposter syndrome. This is when the caregiver doubts themselves or, worse yet, feels defeated. The caregiver pretends to know and fully grasp the physical, mental, financial, and medical situation of the loved one they are caring for and hopes no one will notice. Most will just put on a mask of confidence and competence.

Needles, baths, Hoyer lifts, rollators, wound vacs, wheelchairs, medication management, infusions, meal prep, wigs, shaving . . . sometimes all in the same day! Caregivers do it! Why? Because, today, caregiving encompasses being a nurse, a health advocate, a legal representative, a physical therapist, a bath aide, an occupational therapist, a home remodeler, a housekeeper, a chauffeur, an appointment setter, a secretary, a laundress, a gardener, a librarian, a bookkeeper, a chef, a nutritionist, a therapist, and much more!

Being the caregiver to our parents or our spouse or even an ill or disabled child can create imposter syndrome that manifests in stress, depression, and anxiety, leading to chronic caregiver fatigue. The only way to combat this is to allow room to grow by learning about both yourself and the person you are caring for, and by seeking solutions or resources in order to mitigate the initial crisis and to create needed life balance for the future.

To combat the theory of elasticity and imposter syndrome as it relates to caregiving, I recommend the psychology of Carol S. Dweck in her book *Mindset*. In this work, Dr. Dweck explores two opposite mindsets. One mindset is abundance and growth, and the other is a fixed scarcity mindset suggesting we have limited aptitude and possibilities. The growth mindset suggests one can learn and grow into infinite possibilities. This mindset is much more forgiving and loving toward oneself, allowing positive brain connections to occur to create new pathways, ideas, and understanding. What can caregivers do to stay in this positive frame of mind to allow growth and learning?

Here are five steps to maintain a positive frame of mind when caregiving:

Make time for you to feel like yourself.

Try your best to keep up your hobbies; you just might have to modify it. For me, I like to sing, so I found an outlet to do so. It wasn't a two-hour choir rehearsal and singing at church every Sunday for two more hours, but I could meet friends for an hour and sing some karaoke. If you like reading, facials, bubble baths, walks in the park, working on cars, collecting antiques, shopping, sports or making cards, whatever your fancy, just reimagine it and incorporate happiness into your life and routine. Your brain and everyone around you will thank you.

Embrace the lifelong learner inside you.

Realize that no one on this earth can possibly know everything or know it on command. To walk and speak, we had to learn it. Don't be so hard on yourself. Trust in your higher power and reel in the amazing and multitalented person you are becoming. Every day, you may want to journal or have a conversation about what you learned. Reflecting on that today, next week, and a year from now will give that shot of dopamine you'll need and prove you are growing as a person. Some call this a gratitude journal, but I call it magic!

Reach out to your community—seek support.

Our ego and fear of judgement keep us from asking questions and seeking help. If the information you are looking for could help you or someone else, you need to ask that question. For example, when I spoke to the health care professionals about my mom, I had a list of questions, her recent records, and a full list of her medications. I was ready to say, "Explain that again, as if you're speaking to a fifth grader." I have two master's degrees, which didn't matter when it came to getting the information and options that would help my mom. The questions you ask are out of love and support. Don't ever leave a conversation kicking yourself for not getting clarity. This rule goes when dealing with health care professionals as well as the supporting medical community at large. There are many organizations that exist for the sole purpose of helping people like you and those you love.

Connect with whom you are caring for.

You may think you know a person, especially if it is your own mom, but the time spent together can unveil a gift to rediscover your loved one's favorite memories and life experiences. Storytelling is a wonderful way for both the caregiver and person receiving care to connect, and you may hear something added to the story that changes the version heard. I discovered that my mom first saw my dad on a street corner, pointed to him from a bus window, and proclaimed to her sorority sister, "That's the kind I want, right there." Their love-at-first-sight story was not at all the version I had grown up with. These revelations can deepen relationships, build trust, breed understanding, and allow our synapses to positively charge. Get curious and ask some questions. Your family history might just get rewritten.

Share what works for you.

If you have a tip or a tried-and-true resource that makes your life or the life of the person you are caring for better, it's time to share. Share it with your family, your community, the groups you are involved in, and please share with me. Opening the conversation about how to be the best caregiver is empowering and could positively affect fifty million lives plus the lives they serve.

Review the finances and all insurance.

These are easy tasks to accomplish. Work with someone you know, like, and trust. Ask questions like, "If this was your loved one, what would you suggest?" Work with someone who is unbiased and licensed in your state. Choose a professional who knows you are important and is motivated to make everyone's lives better through their knowledge, inter-action, communication, and character.

What's the driving force for these actions to create better caregivers? It is the willingness to be vulnerable because it leads us to the universal language of love. If the fifty million Americans caregiving for a family member got that dose of love consistently, what a difference the mental health of our country would experience! Be the change, grow beyond measure, love more, then love more deeply, honor yourself, and honor your family. Hold your head up and hold the hand of your loved one. Someday you will want the same from the caregiver who holds your hand.

Recognized as a leading producer in life and health insurance nationwide, Diane Finnestead advocates health reform through National Association Health Underwriters serving on the St. Louis board, the Missouri board, as well as their National Speaker's Bureau. She credits her ability to help thousands of Americans find the right insurance over the past twenty-plus years to her background and career in education.

Diane speaks from the heart, whether it's virtual or as a stage speaker for conferences, summits, podcasts, radio shows, and webinars on the topics of health insurance, Medicare, entrepreneurship, business and "Giving the Care Back to the Caregiver."

Diane holds a bachelor's degree in Music from the University of North Texas, and two master's degrees from Webster University. She currently lives and works in both St. Louis, Missouri, and Folly Beach, South Carolina.

To receive your free updated copy of the "Caregiver's Resource List" please reach out to Diane at…

314-302-5743

www.youtube.com/watch?v=SE9-gvv3yBM (video interview)

agents@dianeinsurancestl.com

www.dianeinsurancestl.com

www.linkedin.com/in/diane-finnestead-mat-Ed-s-4187912a/

www.Facebook.com/dianeinsurancestl

Beth Oseroff

Tossing Out Society's Checklist

When asked to write about growth, I chuckled to myself. Have I "grown" enough to write about the concept of growth? Don't I still have a lot of "growing up" to do? Ultimately, I decided, what better way to continue to grow than to try something new?

I can remember as a young kid being asked, "What do you want to be when you grow up?" That answer often changed. In kindergarten my answer was, "I don't want to grow up, I want to be little forever." Sometime in elementary school, after watching daytime television on a sick day, I decided I wanted to be Judge Judy. This aspiration has stuck with me, although I have no interest in gaining my law degree or being in a court room—I found out in middle school history class that it would be way too much reading for me. But to an elementary school girl in the late '90s, Judge Judy was one of the few powerful women displayed in the media. At ten years of age, I had no clue what the court cases were about, but I did know that Judge Judy was in charge and was well respected by those in her courtroom, and that is what I aspired to be.

As a young girl on a mission to "be in charge," I was often put down or reprimanded for being bossy, or talking too much, or oversharing my opinion. I was the oldest sibling with two younger brothers. My parents separated toward the end of elementary school, and in my eyes I was taking over my courtroom, controlling my own narrative, which meant everyone else should live within the confines of my narrative too.

As I grew, so did my confidence; but stepping onto William Woods University's campus as a freshman was one of the most nerve-racking experiences of my life. I wish I could have whispered into that girl's ear, "Don't worry so much about how other people look at you—you will make mistakes, you will learn from them, and don't forget to have some fun."

I was excited. I was in a new town with new people, and no one assumed anything about me. No one knew that my dad wasn't in the picture, or that I wasn't the richest girl at school. For the first time I had the ability to create my own narrative. I wasn't sure what I wanted to be, but at first look it was a sorority girl, so off to rush I went.

Sorority recruitment was the first time in my life that I put myself out there and was rejected. I realized I needed to create something for myself as an individual, and by the sixth week of school I was a University Ambassador, elected as a freshman representative to the university's Student Alumni Council, and was chosen to show one of the top horses in the equestrian program. I was well on my way to becoming my own Judge Judy. In between first and second semester, I applied to be a Resident Advisor (RA). I now know that job would define the rest of my college career.

As an RA I had to learn how to gain the respect of my peers, and not just because I had the title but because they respected me and my rules and boundaries. To do my job well, I drew a clear line in the sand of what my boundaries were when it came to things like partying. But to maintain being well liked I drew no lines when it came to doing things for others, which often turned into getting taken advantage of as the sober driver, or as the person who would always "share" their homework assignments, or even as the proverbial punching bag for friends' emotions. I was trying so desperately to take charge of my own courtroom, but unlike Judge Judy, I didn't want anyone to be mad at me or not like my opinion. I had learned how to speak up when I knew what I was saying was right, or fact, or popular opinion, but I was still figuring out what my own voice sounded like.

Throughout graduate school my peers who had "gone out into the world" were finding love and getting married. At this time in our lives, the idea of growing up was about choosing a partner and starting a family. That's when my bridesmaid tour began. By the time I was twenty-six, I had been a bridesmaid five times. Being a bridesmaid is a great honor, but the constant questions from parents, friends, and family of "When will it be you?" gets old fast. I was still trying to answer the question of what I wanted to be when I grew up.

Grad school came and went, and I was still far from being Judge Judy, so I did what was comfortable and stayed in Fulton, Missouri, not too far from my bubble at William Woods. I worked on finding my professional voice in a new director role at the local YMCA. I learned about development and fundraising and the daily tasks that are required for growth—growth in membership, growth in scholarship dollars, growth in community and grant support. In this time, I also grew as an individual, one who could stand on my own two feet and support myself. Growing up, I always knew that I needed to be financially stable on my own, and for the first time in my life, I was. That was growth.

After eight years in Fulton and three with the YMCA, I made the hard decision to move away and join the staff of the American Heart Association in St. Louis. I had finally answered the question of what profession I wanted to have when I grew up, yet I found myself feeling like I was still a couple of bullet points behind on society's checklist.

In March of 2020, almost a year and a half after I moved to St. Louis, a global pandemic helped me toss the checklist out the door and create my own. I have no family in St. Louis, so as my friends were going to stay with their parents, creating their quarantine pods, I was all alone—an outgoing extrovert's absolute worst nightmare.

This forced stop was a pivotal moment. As someone who's constantly moving, I have learned that to grow, you must stop. I had never really been into self-help books or journaling, but I needed something to do with my time, and a radio personality I listened to was starting a dating self-help journal and I thought, "What do I have to lose?" This thing that started as a silly endeavor ended up changing my frame of reference for "growing up." I, of course, drafted one of my best friends to do it too, and we set out on a fourteen-week journey.

Each week and each chapter we learned something new about ourselves. By the end of the fourteen weeks, I came to know what should be on my life checklist, and to be proud of the things that I had already checked off, instead of being ashamed of the things society thought I hadn't.

Timing is everything. Four months after finishing the self-help dating book, I went on my last first date. I had been on more first dates than I could count. I had just moved, we were still in a global pandemic, and it was February, which meant a patio in the freezing cold. I did not want to go. My friends pushed me to go, and thank goodness I did, because now we have set our wedding date—requiring a whole new checklist and creating a whole new courtroom, where I suppose there are two judges and members of the jury.

When I think back on the little girl who aspired to be Judge Judy, I often think of all the things that could have gone differently. I thought growing meant reinventing myself to fit into a box or to be what society thought, that to be grown up meant that I needed to be in charge or the most well liked in the room. But I had it all backward. To grow, you need to know what is important to you: what your values are, what your passions are, what success looks like to you, who you need to surround yourself with, and the steps to take to complete that vision...always knowing that the vision may change.

When we are asked what we want to be in kindergarten, growth seems like something we are striving to achieve, and once you have made it, then you are done. But why be done? Why not keep asking yourself, "What do I want to be? Who do I want to be? How do I want to keep growing and learning?" So maybe, after all, the kindergarten version of me was right in saying I don't want to grow up—but not necessarily because I want to be little forever, but because I don't want to ever stop growing.

Beth Oseroff, originally from Dallas, TX, is a Senior Development Director at the American Heart Association (AHA) in St. Louis, MO. Beth earned her BS in Sports Management and MBA with at concentration in Entrepreneurial Leadership from William Woods University. In her work with the American Heart Association, Beth works with volunteers and leaders across the St. Louis metro to raise funds and awareness for the lifesaving mission of the AHA. In 2021 Beth was awarded the AHA's Excellence in Fundraising award for her work.

Beth loves to travel and in her free time can be found enjoying time with family and friends. She is excited about the year ahead as she is newly engaged to her fiancé, Walter, and is planning a wedding for May of 2023.

Beth.Oseroff@gmail.com
www.linkedin.com/in/bethoseroff/
www.instagram.com/betho1112/

The next book in the
Deconstructing G.R.I.T. Collection,

RESILIENCE

will launch in January 2023.

For information about how
You can <u>SHARE YOUR STORY</u> in
the next books in our series ...

INTENTION

&

TENACITY

Please contact me at
jennifer@gritcollect.com

Jennifer Bardot

"Nothing happens until something moves."

— Albert Einstein

JAMIE WEAVER
Senior Client Development Specialist
& Dabbler in Grass Roots Marketing

Weaverjamie78@gmail
618-250-9669

facebook.com/jamie.weaver.18
linkedin.com/in/jamie-weaver-21bab3124

Made in the USA
Monee, IL
24 February 2023

28617616R00154